AFRICAN AMERICANS of Chattanooga

African Americans *of* Chattanooga

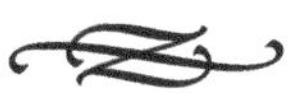

A History of Unsung Heroes

Rita Lorraine Hubbard

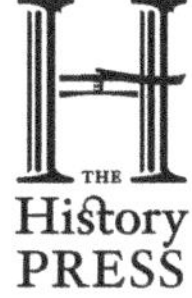

Published by The History Press
Charleston, SC 29403
www.historypress.net

First published 2007

Manufactured in the United States

ISBN 978.1.59629.315.1

Library of Congress Cataloging-in-Publication Data

Hubbard, Rita L.
African Americans of Chattanooga : a history of unsung heroes / Rita L. Hubbard.
p. cm.
Includes bibliographical references.
ISBN-13: 978-1-59629-315-1 (alk. paper)
1. African Americans--Tennessee--Chattanooga--History. 2. African Americans--Tennessee--Chattanooga--Biography. 3. Chattanooga (Tenn.)--History. 4. Chattanooga (Tenn.)--Biography. I. Title.
F444.C49N44 2007
976.8'820092396073--dc22
[B]
2007038710

Contents

Special Dedication

Bishop W.C. Hunter

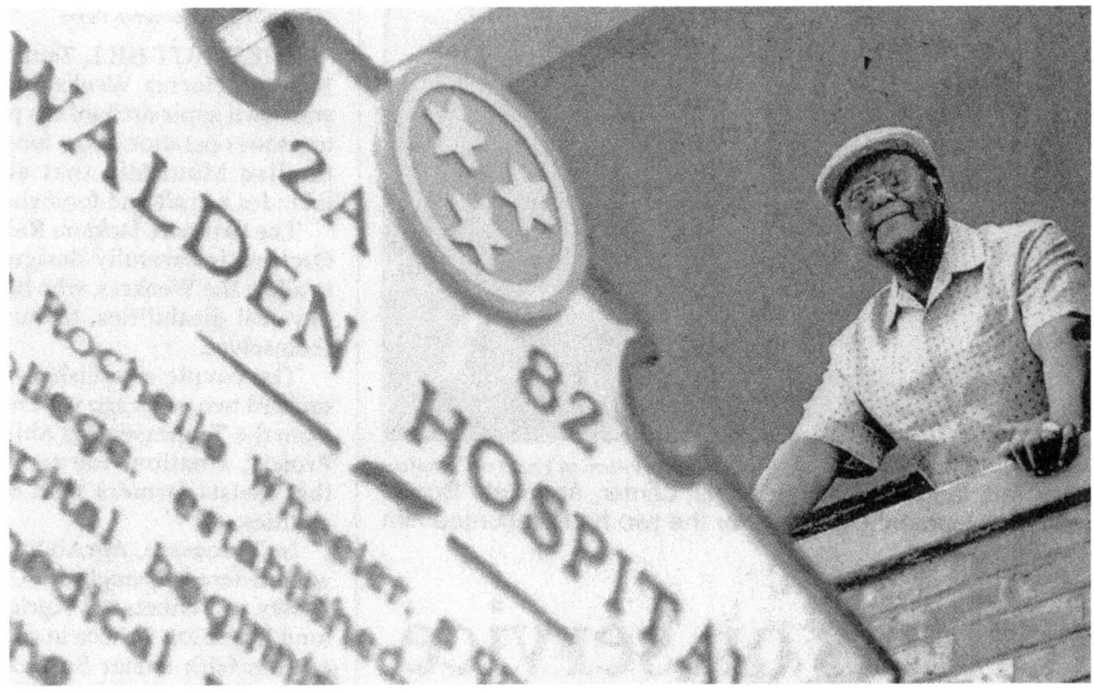

This book is dedicated to pastor, philanthropist, entrepreneur and author, Bishop W.C. Hunter, who saw the value in the old Walden Hospital—Chattanooga, Tennessee's first and only African American teaching hospital—and did not let the torch go out. He generously allowed me (and others) to participate in Walden's glorious revival, and during the peak of that excitement, he wisely suggested that I write a book about African Americans in Chattanooga. I am keenly aware that without the invitation he extended to me, and without his sage suggestion to bring light to Chattanooga's half-hidden African American history, this book would most probably never have been written.

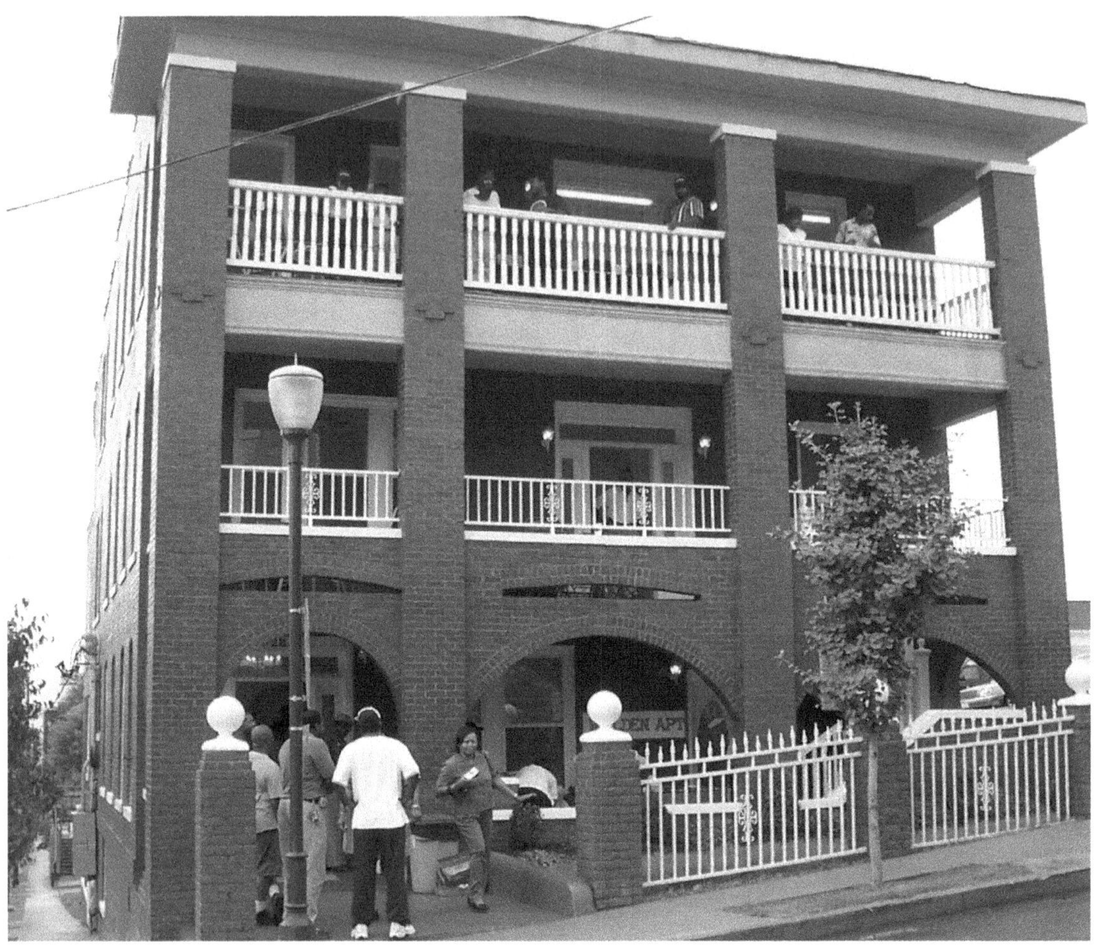

In addition to his revitalization of the old Walden Hospital, Bishop Hunter was the first and only African American in Chattanooga to build an amusement park with personal funds, as well as the first and only African American in Chattanooga to build and run a bottling company for his original barbecue sauce recipe. In August 2007, he was one of several persons honored by the Tennessee Multicultural Chamber of Commerce as being a "Chattanooga Legend." He is truly a remarkable man.

Above: Walden Hospital was renovated by philanthropist and entrepreneur W.C. Hunter, and was rededicated as the Walden Apartments. The grand reopening was held on July 8, 2003. *Photograph courtesy of Annetta Arnold, ©2003.*

Previous page: This is a *Chattanooga Times* photograph of philanthropist and entrepreneur, W.C. Hunter, who purchased the crumbling Walden Hospital building and renovated it into modern apartments. The building was rededicated as the Walden Apartments on July 8, 2003. Hunter is also responsible for the creation of this book.

Preface

Even though African Americans have played a vital role in virtually every phase of Tennessee history, they have traditionally had to settle for creating a separate historical documentation of their contributions. It is an undisputed fact that African Americans have fought for freedom, served as wilderness guides, labored as slaves and forged paths as early educators and politicians, and yet still today little is actually documented or understood about the roles they played.

In reading the works of such historians as Lester C. Lamon and E. Raymond Evans, I have gained much insight into the volume of work that has already been done to reveal the importance of Tennessee African Americans, and I have come to understand that an even greater volume of work remains to be done. That being said, it is not the purpose of this book to offer lengthy, detail-laden passages about the blow-by-blow accomplishments of Chattanooga African Americans. Rather, this book builds upon the work that has already begun and strikes the next blow that will scratch more of the surface of African American presence in Chattanooga and lead the way for yet more detailed study.

I have, of course, drawn heavily upon the in-depth research of newspapers, early books and other historical sources, but I freely admit that there are noticeable gaps in this historical record. It is my hope that readers will study and enjoy the information I have been able to provide rather than point out those portions that, for whatever reason, do not appear in this first volume.

Acknowledgements

I wish to thank the following persons for their patience, encouragement and assistance while I labored with this volume:

Bishop W.C. Hunter
Commissioner (ret.) John Franklin
Sherrie Gilchrist, President and CEO, Tennessee Multicultural Chamber of Commerce
Josephine Wheeler and Bette Wheeler-Strictland, family of the late Dr. Emma Rochelle Wheeler
Michael Jones, Manager of Minority and Women-Owned Business Development and EPB of Chattanooga
Lisa Jones, Chattanooga Police Department
Darla Brock and Karina McDaniel, Tennessee State Library & Archives (TSLA)
Jim Reece, Karen Myrick, Suzette Raney, April Mitchell and Mary Helms, of the Chattanooga-Hamilton County Bicentennial Library, Local Genealogy Department
William F. "Bill" Hull and the Chattanooga Regional History Museum
Mr. Billy Weeks, *Chattanooga Times*
Library of Congress Prints and Photographs
Timothy Connelly, Director, NARA/NHPRC
University of North Carolina at Chapel Hill
Linda Wynn, Tennessee Historical Commission
The late Vilma Fields, Chattanooga African American History Museum
Jim Ogden, Marie Paris and the staff of the Chickamauga-Chattanooga National Military Park (Chickamauga Battlefield)
Charles Hunter IV, thank you for your generosity
I apologize for any names omitted

Part I

Early History

Negroes measure their progress and contribution to the community, state, and nation, not by the heights to which they have risen, but by the depths from whence they have come.

One hundred years ago they were slaves...today they are living side by side with the children of their former masters, working diligently to make the south and the nation at large a better place for their having been set free and given opportunity.

Thrift and industry had to be theirs, despite the lack of intelligence and the lack of literacy. They were the mechanics of the south. They cut the stone from the quarry, made the bricks, felled the trees and hewed them into dwellings, shod the horses and otherwise learned to work with their hands and to build.

Here in Chattanooga, we have various instances of how even before freedom came, Negroes "let their buckets down where they were" and set about to make definite and honorable contributions...

—Excerpt from "From Slavery...Negroes' Progress," by Jasper T. Duncan in Chattanooga Times, *September 1938.*

1.

Early History of African Americans in Tennessee

There is reason to believe that African Americans were in Tennessee territory as early as the year 1541. This was when Hernando De Soto's Spanish expedition traveled along the Tennessee River in search of precious gold. It is presumed by many historians that De Soto had Negroes with him when he camped near Memphis, and even when he stopped in the area that would later become known as Chattanooga, Tennessee, because it is known that he had them with him when he originally left Spain.

Unfortunately, it would be many, many years before white Americans considered African Americans important enough to record their names and biographies for their descendants to track. Typically, only first names appeared in early documentation; everything else about the African American, including his very existence, was typically ignored.

In the 1600s, the Tennessee River became an important part of the French trade route. The French quickly recognized that trading with the American Indians would prove very prosperous for them, so they established trading posts all along the Tennessee River. Of course the English had already studied the many benefits that the Tennessee River had to offer and they too wanted control of this trade route. The result was the French and Indian War. The French sent an army of 1,200 white men and 2,400 American Indians and Negroes to take up quarters at Fort Assumption on the bluff of Memphis. At the end of the French and Indian War the English won control over trade in the area. But for the purposes of tracing African American presence, this documentation proves that Negroes were in the Tennessee area in these early times.

In 1766, a colonel by the name of James Smith and a group of long hunters came to Tennessee to explore the Cumberland County. The colonel brought his mulatto lad "Jim" with him. The colonel was impressed enough with "Jim" to devote an entire stanza to him in his diary.

In 1779, a man by the name of James Robertson came from the Holston settlement to explore the site that is now called Nashville, Tennessee. Robertson brought what he called simply "a Negro fellow" with him, the only reference given to another early African American who set foot on Tennessee soil. This "Negro fellow" helped explore and select Fort Nashborough, the early name for Nashville, Tennessee.

Of course, new settlers were coming to Tennessee all the time and many of them brought Negroes with them to help settle the land. By the time the first official census was taken in 1790 there were already 3,417 slaves in the Tennessee territory.

It did not take long for the number of Negroes to begin to make a steady rise. By the time Tennessee became a state in 1796, there were 10,613 slaves in the total population of 77,282 Tennessee citizens. Then, when invention of the cotton gin boosted the cotton industry to unheard of levels of recognition, slavery expanded quickly and widely, especially between the years 1790 and 1835.

Some historians say that the Tennessee slave was generally more mentally developed than slaves from other states. This was because most of the Tennessee farmers owned only small estates and they had much more interaction with their slaves and gave them more diverse responsibilities.

The Eastern Tennessee slaves, such as those near Chattanooga and in the Hamilton County area, were thought to have a much harsher existence than slaves in most other slaveholding states. But whatever their condition was in the beginning, they made the most of their surroundings and left an impact on the city, the state and in some cases, the country.

EARLY ACTIVITY IN CHATTANOOGA—1820–1865

While concentrated efforts to settle the state were being made in other areas of Tennessee, things were also happening in the little town that would eventually become known as Chattanooga. In 1816—and even earlier than that—traders would stop at the little landing on the riverfront and trade with a man by the name of John Ross, who also happened to be chief of the Cherokee American Indians. This was how the name Ross's Landing came into existence.

By the time Hamilton County was created by action of the State of Tennessee on October 25, 1819, there were already sixteen free Negroes and thirty-nine slaves in the city.

1820s

In the 1820s, Thomas Crutchfield—an early white Chattanooga settler—and his father-in-law, Samuel Clegg, were the leading contractors in Southeast Tennessee. Their names are mentioned in this historical volume because some of the earliest recordings of African American activity in Chattanooga are associated with these names.

Crutchfield established his family in a two-story log home near Pine and West 9th Streets. There were several outlying huts near Crutchfield's home for his slaves. This Crutchfield settlement became known as "The Cabins."

Crutchfield also owned a brickyard on Water Street (1st Street) near the Tennessee River. Nearly seventy African Americans worked in Crutchfield's brickyard. One slave in particular, known as "Yellow Bill" because of his complexion, also worked in the brickyard.

Yellow Bill and another slave named Mills Crutchfield were foremen of the brickyard. Yellow Bill's skill and character inspired Crutchfield's trust, and he often allowed Yellow Bill to go about the area without supervision to do large jobs.

According to records—and typical of the times—none of the slaves could read or write, but Yellow Bill understood construction figures and could work from crude types of plans used during that day. The rest of the slaves made bricks by digging out an area and hauling water from the river to pour into the area. They then used oxen to tramp the mud.

1840s

By 1840, the 183,057 slaves held in bondage in Tennessee were valued at $550 a head. Hamilton County's population of 8,175 included 584 slaves and 93 free Negroes. One of these free Negroes was a wealthy blacksmith and wagon maker named "Uncle Bill," who serviced almost every citizen of Chattanooga. His story will be told in a later section of this book.

Chattanooga was still a very small settlement, but it was by all means a bustling one. Several times a day stagecoaches came and went to Knoxville and Nashville, which was once called Fort Nashborough. Ross's Landing was the center for trade for a large portion of Hamilton County and beyond. Of course, there was no bridge to connect the north side of the settlement to the Ross's Landing side, so the people came and went by flatboats and rafts for their needed supplies.

1841 Records

A prominent white family with the McCallie surname left Washington for Chattanooga, Tennessee, in March 1841. When they finally arrived, McCallie settled his family on twenty-five acres of land on the east end of town. The McCallie name is mentioned in this historical volume because there are further records of early African American activity associated with the name.

The McCallies planted a portion of their twenty-five acres in orchards. They owned two men and three women slaves, and they put them to work cultivating the peaches, apples, plums and other fruits in the orchard. These slaves lived in small houses situated behind the large McCallie home.

Unlike the typical slave owner of that day, Mrs. McCallie preferred to teach her slaves to read. She also believed in religion and brought her slaves to church with her. The McCallie name still survives in the twenty-first century. In fact, "the road coming into Chattanooga past the McCallie property from the old Brainerd Mission across Missionary Ridge"[1] would first take the name of McCallie Road, and later would be known as McCallie Avenue.

1844

Details about the lives of African Americans in Chattanooga are sketchy in the early years, and are not easy to come by. However, it is known that during the 1844 presidential election in which James K. Polk of Tennessee opposed Henry Clay, one political enthusiast from Chattanooga came into town with what was termed a large group of Negroes of all ages. They performed a political song about Polk and Clay, and it is said that the performance put the entire town of Chattanooga in an uproar because it was so unusual and so well-done.

Unfortunately, early African Americans were like shadows in a field; they were a people whose lives, loves and backgrounds were considered too unimportant to document. In this case, their performance was recorded for history, but their names and personal identities were completely omitted.

1849

By the late 1840s, more of the townspeople owned slaves and trading in slaves was fairly common in Chattanooga. In fact, a man by the name of F.A. Parham offered various lots of land for sale, and he always made it a point to remind his clients that he would take either cash or Negroes in payment for the land.

There is also documentation of a constable's sale at the market house in Chattanooga, which notified the public of a Negro girl who was to be auctioned off to the highest bidder.

Lastly, there is documentation that A.H. Johnston & Company had an office on Market Street, opposite the W&A Depot, and Johnston engaged professionally in the traffic of slaves.

1853–1854

Legislature often placed rigid restrictions on slaves, free Negroes and those who in some way or other were involved with both. In Chattanooga, the legislature taxed slave traders $500 annually for the privilege of selling slaves. Unfortunately, those African Americans who were freeborn or newly-freed were not simply left to live their lives in peace. They were required to pay taxes for the privilege of being and remaining free. Free persons of color paid a head tax of $5 annually for each male, and $3 annually for each female. They were also required to register with the city recorder and show proof of their freedom. If they could not pay their fees or produce proof of their freedom, they were "deemed to be slaves" and were promptly dealt with as such.

In Chattanooga, those Negroes who remained in a state of bondage were very strictly regulated by ordinance. They could not remain in Chattanooga's town square at night or over weekends unless they actually lived in Chattanooga, and even if they did, they had to have the express permission of their owners or employers to remain in the town. Fear of what they might be thinking or planning was always at the forefront of their owners' minds. Therefore they could not gather in groups for any purpose except public worship, and even then, this worship must be done under the strict supervision of white people.

The 1860s and the Civil War

By the year 1860, the population of Chattanooga/Hamilton County had grown to an impressive 2,545. There were 457 Negroes on record, of which 93 were free.

These freemen were involved in various occupations; some were blacksmiths and some were day laborers, but most were farmhands, washerwomen, seamstresses and draymen.

By the time the question of slavery, freedom and the Civil War was put to the townspeople, Chattanooga was really still a fairly new community. It had only come into existence (as Ross's Landing) in 1816, and Hamilton County had only been established in 1819. This meant that this small community had been in existence for a mere forty-two years when "the Question" was raised. The majority of Chattanooga citizens were small, simple farmers who had very little cash income, and as a whole they disliked the wealthy plantation-owning aristocratic classes. They wanted slavery abolished—not so much because they were opposed to slavery, but because they were opposed to unemployment. After all, cheap or free Negro labor was a threat to their very livelihood, and so more than anything they wanted an end to slavery so that they could have their own chance in the employment market. They wanted to see the Negroes set free, but only if the Negroes were completely removed from the American scene to make way for the poorer white class.

February 1862

For the most part, Chattanooga was initially on the side of the Confederacy when the Civil War began. Even though the battle was late reaching the Chattanooga valley, the citizens were still eager to do their own part to preserve what they believed were their personal rights. Therefore, when news came that 1,200 or so sick and convalescent Confederate soldiers were being evacuated from Nashville, Tennessee, the citizens of Chattanooga sprang into action. In February 1862 the townspeople organized a "force" of Negro men and women that was put to work cleaning buildings, which would serve as hospitals for the sick and injured. This was the very first experience Chattanooga citizens had with the Civil War. This was also the first experience they had with formal hospitals. Their initial part in the war was to hastily make these buildings available for use as convalescent hospitals, and free Negroes and slaves alike were expected to help in the effort.

By the time the full threat of war made its way to Chattanooga, a sudden fear and suspicion of all African Americans swept through the city. Most of the African Americans in the city had been in the area since the very beginning, but rumors about revolts were circulating all over the South and like other white communities, Chattanooga's white population quickly adopted a curfew law. This new law prohibited any African American—whether free or bound—from being "abroad in the city after 7:30 p.m."

Winter 1863–1864

By 1864, Chattanooga had undergone an overwhelming military siege. Just like the familiar storyline of *Gone with the Wind* by Margaret Mitchell, Chattanooga's food supply was ravished by the Union forces. Everyday commodities like milk were almost unheard of, and it became an art and a chore to figure out how to keep the few livestock that were still in the area alive.

Those few people fortunate enough to still have living, breathing livestock had to feed them hard tack—the horrid military food that the soldiers ate, which was so often laughed at and joked about in personal diaries. This, unfortunately, was barely enough to keep them breathing. In fact, food of any type was so hard to come by that the mules in the area had to live off of "wagon tongues and fence rails."[2]

Conditions were not much better for the humans. Butter and cheese were considered luxuries during the winter of 1863, and it was practically impossible to locate fruit of any sort. Bacon was available, but only barely, and what bread could be thrown together had to be prepared without milk or yeast in it.

Following the Battle of Missionary Ridge, Federal forces remained in camp all around Chattanooga, and the city was transformed into a tent city. There were tents of every size and every type: soldiers' tents, business tents and tents for the African Americans—who were now called "Freedmen."

Most of the African Americans who lived in Chattanooga from 1861 to 1865 found work as government employees, particularly in the Commissary Department. Those who weren't government employees served as cooks and hostlers for both Union and the Confederate armies.

Summer 1864

As the war dragged on, refugees began appearing all over Chattanooga. There were both black and white refugees and wanderers, and all of them were in a most destitute condition. Everybody—black and white—came to Chattanooga in search of food and safety. They continued to flood into the city and by October 1864 the city was full to bursting with traders, adventurers, soldiers, poor whites, refugees and African Americans.

November 1864

By November, Chattanooga reported a staggering 3,893 refugees in the city limits. In fact, the number of African American refugees was estimated to be equal to the total number of African Americans serving in the military in the entire Chattanooga area. This influx of African Americans found shelter wherever they could, but especially along the river.

Of historical note is the fact that many of the original white families of Chattanooga fled the city during the Union occupation. By 1865, various white families returned, but when they arrived most of them had nothing. After all, their Confederate money was no good and their Negro labor was gone, and those who were once landowners found that their lands now belonged to the people and governments of the North.

In contrast, the African Americans who had served with the Union forces had money to spend, and they used this money to purchase "finery" for their own families. Many of these African Americans took advantage of the plight of the returning whites by buying whole wardrobes from them. They also purchased their furniture and bought uniforms from the destitute whites.

November 7, 1865, Census

By late 1865, the Civil War was over and there were 900 Negro males, 930 females and 827 children in the African American community. There were also another estimated 3,500 Negroes living on the other side of the river, which would later become known as North Chattanooga. These North Chattanooga African Americans had built a village of huts there, which became known as "Contraband."

According to Chattanooga record books, maintaining law and order was extremely difficult after the Civil War ended. The composition of the city had changed, and there were many refugees, white and black, who were from places and situations completely opposite of what Chattanooga was used to. There were also returning ex-Confederate soldiers who had been mustered out of the service or released from Federal prisons, and there were Federal troops who had little regard for the Chattanooga they had conquered. There were even aimless camp followers who had fled some other plantation or bondage, and who now roamed the countryside free to do as they pleased. These new citizens of Chattanooga proved to be unpredictable and dangerous—so much so that visitors to the city were subjected to unprecedented violence. Because of all this chaos and uncertainty, two important events occurred: Chattanooga City set up a volunteer police force composed of the citizens of the town to help control the new bad element; and the Freedmen's Bureau was established.

The Freedmen's Bureau's primary goals were to help aid refugees, keep down lawlessness and act as an employment agency for the newly freed African Americans, who found themselves suddenly homeless, jobless and landless. The Freedmen's Bureau soon secured employment for approximately three thousand of the Chattanooga African Americans by sending them to work on the plantations that were now in the possession of the Northern men of the Mississippi Valley. But the bureau could not find employment for everyone. There were another estimated three thousand African Americans who were jobless.

Jobless though they were, these African Americans did not sit idly by. They might live in tents and barely scrape by, but they were now free to progress. It did not take long for progress—and a great deal of it—to spread through the community.

The Reconstruction Period

Tennessee's black population had never been so large that it threatened white control of state politics, so African Americans—especially those in Chattanooga—had their own period of "reconstruction." They voted freely during the late nineteenth century and produced a small, steady supply of legislators and local officials.[3] In fact, the Chattanooga area was described as a "most favorable political climate" for black officials.

The Chattanooga African American population sprang into action almost as soon as slavery ended. According to an early historical account penned by J. Bliss White, "the smoke of battle had hardly cleared away before they began to purchase property and establish homes among the pioneers."[4] Among these early enterprisers were such

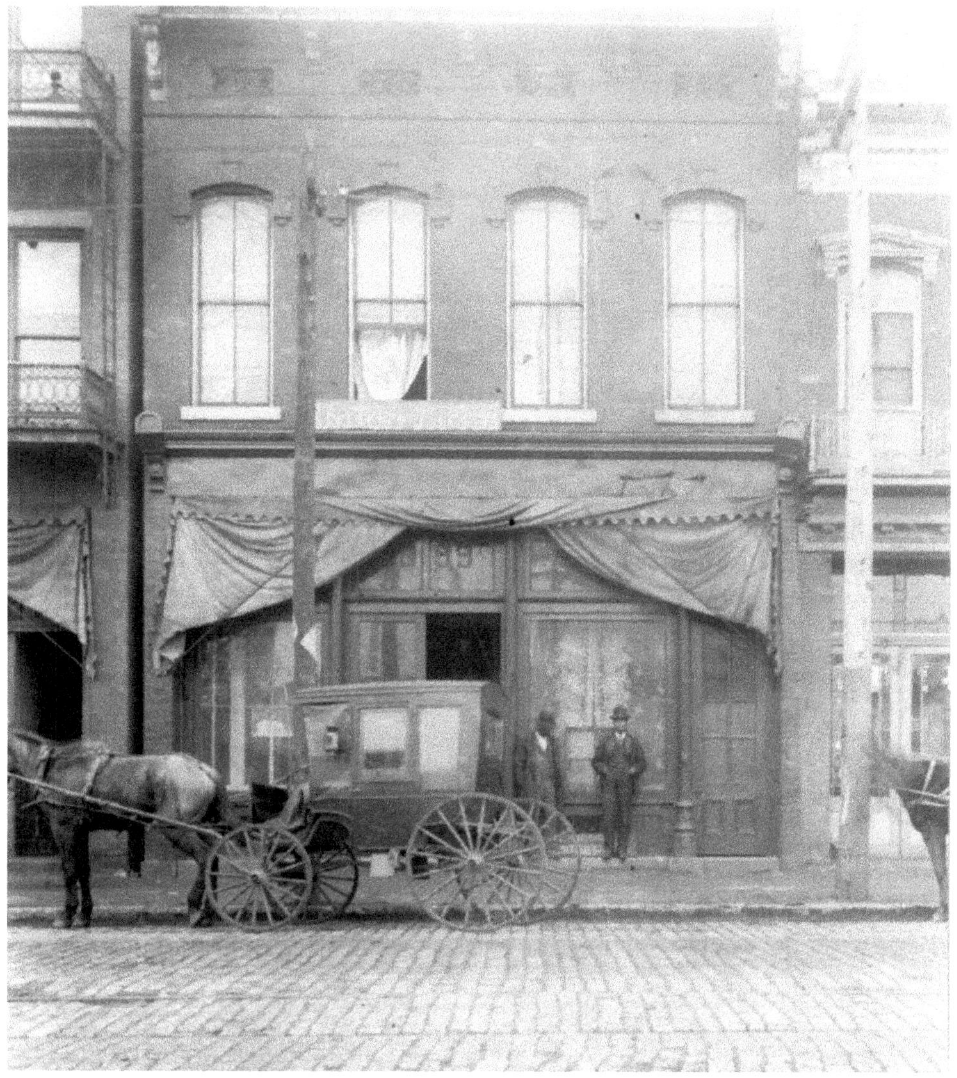

An 1899 photograph of the old Union Hotel, located on what appears to be 9th Street, although this has not been verified. This photograph was displayed as a part of the African American Negro Exhibit at the Paris exposition of 1900. *Photograph courtesy of the Library of Congress Prints and Photographs, ©1899.*

men as the Reverend Harrison H. Huston, Jeff Cooley, John Tolliver and George W. Sewell, the veteran barber. Of course, except for George Sewell, whose photograph and activities have been documented, the deeds and daring of these men have been lost to time. Their names are mentioned here because they appeared in the early works of J. Bliss White.

By 1867, Chattanooga African Americans were actively taking part in city government. Mr. Esquire Flowers became the first "colored" man to be elected as a member of the county court in 1867. Of course, another account—noted in both the *Chattanooga Times* and the book, *Men of Mark: Eminent, Progressive and Rising* by George

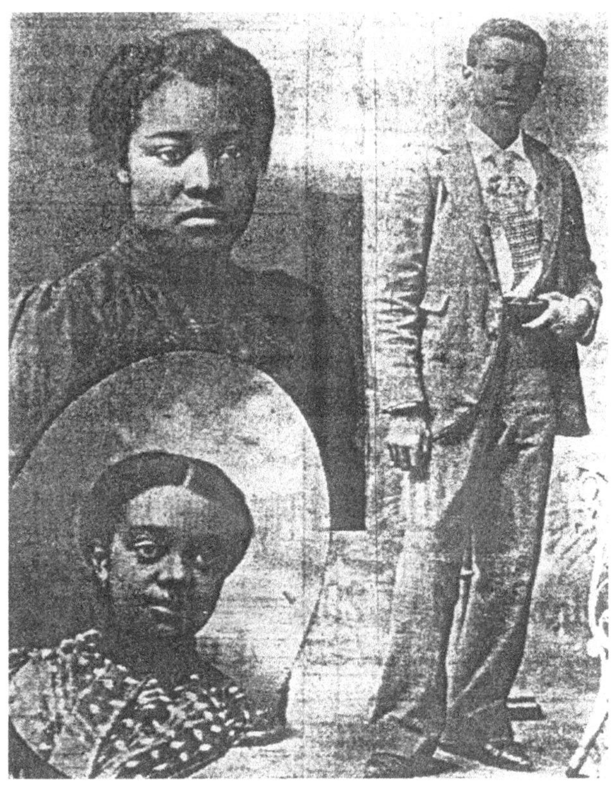

A faded newspaper photograph of an early group of Howard High School graduates. *Photograph courtesy of the* Chattanooga Times, *1900.*

M. Rewell—lists John James Irvine as the first African American male elected to the county court. The distinction may be in the fact that Esq. Flowers was simply elected to the court, whereas John James Irvine was elected as county clerk. Nevertheless, both men were listed as being "firsts" in the county court.

C.P. Letcher went on record as being the very first Negro in Chattanooga to sit on the Board of Aldermen in 1868.[5] He was followed two years later by the Reverend Clem Shaw, who represented his own ward in 1870.[6] Other men who held responsible city and county positions included Jim Hodge, Larkin Fralix, Marion Keith, Charley Bird (who later became a policeman), William Richardson, Isaac Allen and Woodson Weaver.

Of a certainty, this obscure little southern African American community, which would at some time or other mysteriously earn itself the unshakeable label of being "a backward city with backward people," was actually highly motivated and civic minded, and was in many ways more progressive than most other Southern communities. These African Americans served with volunteer fire companies, as postal clerks and as justices of the peace and poor commissioners—even in the years before the judicial edicts that came down from Washington demanded that they be included in such occupations.

They even served on the board of education, overseeing the growing educational community that had an encouraging thirty-five children on the segregated school roster and two classroom teachers on the payroll—including the well-known Mrs. Tena Grant-Gilmore.[7]

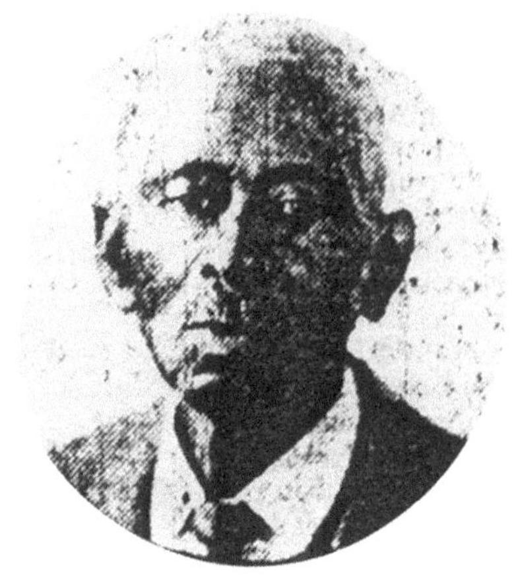

The new freedmen of Chattanooga were active in various arenas. In 1880, these hardworking Chattanooga African Americans helped to cut out Chattanooga's first railroad—the old East Tennessee-Alabama-Georgia. In that same year, four African Americans served on a ten-man police force, and by 1881, seven of the twelve-man Chattanooga police force were African Americans.[8] Included in these numbers were Charley Bird, George White and Andy Thompson. Although not much is known about White, it is known that Bird served as a politician before he became a policeman.

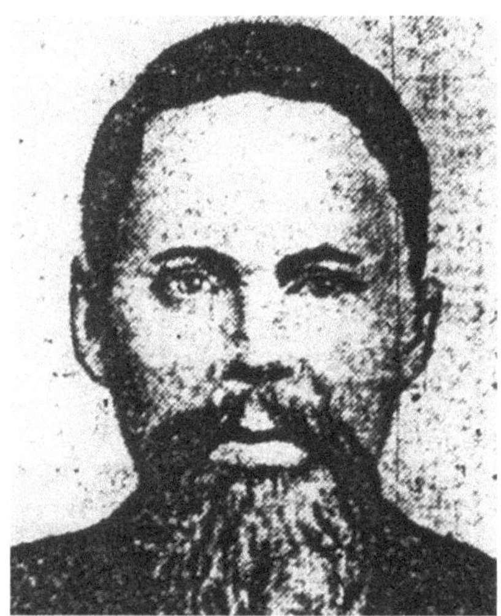

Andy Thompson on the other hand lived an active, well-documented life. An 1896 *Chattanooga Times* article stated that he was once considered the leader of the African American community and held various public offices, beginning with his career in the police department. He even served as captain of the "colored" fire department.[9] Thompson was a member of the Board of Mayor and Aldermen in 1888–89, and represented the fourth ward. He was also in charge of Chattanooga City's chain gang and supervised their cleaning assignments.[10]

In 1882, John James Irvine, who as stated above would eventually become the first African American to be elected to the Hamilton County Circuit Court as clerk (1886), had just been nominated as constable of the Fourteenth Civil District in Hamilton County.[11] Hinton D. Alexander, one of the original Fisk Jubilee Singers and Chattanooga's

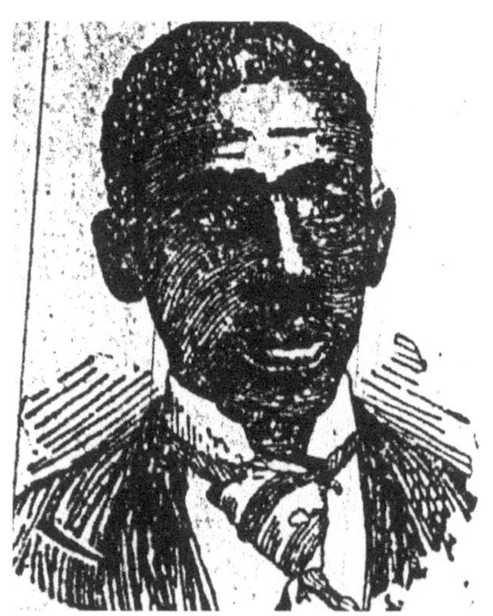

Top: Charley Bird, one of seven African American policemen serving on the Chattanooga police force in the early 1800s. *Photograph courtesy of the* Chattanooga Times, *July 1, 1928, Jubilee No. 25.*

Middle:This is an early photograph of George White, one of seven African American policemen serving on the Chattanooga police force in the early 1800s. *Photograph courtesy of the* Chattanooga Times, *July 1, 1928, Jubilee No. 25.*

Bottom: This is a faded drawing of Andy F. Thompson, an African American who began his career as a Chattanooga policeman in 1880 and rose to the position of captain of the Colored Fire Department. *Photograph courtesy of the* Chattanooga Times, *1896.*

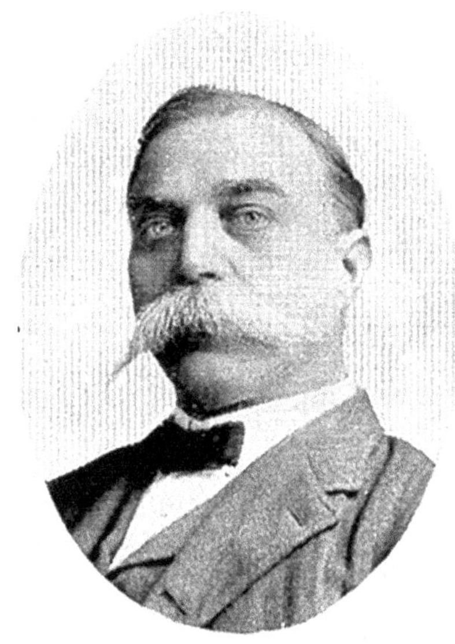

This is a photograph of Hyram Tyree, alderman and deputy sheriff of Hamilton County. Tyree was said to be a man who never lost an opportunity to aid in the development of the African American race. *Photograph courtesy of* 1904 Biography and Achievements of the Colored Citizens of Chattanooga *by J. Bliss White.*

first Negro to go to college, was already working as a letter carrier and was preparing himself to serve the *Chattanooga Times* building in the same capacity the following year. And Attorney Styles Linton Hutchins, the first African American ever admitted to the Georgia Bar, had joined other bold, forward-thinking African Americans of that time in organizing and establishing the *Independent Age* newspaper—the only paper with press and outfit owned and operated entirely by African American men in Chattanooga. By 1886, Hutchins and another Chattanooga Negro—William C. Hodge—would be two of only twelve African Americans who would serve in the Tennessee legislature.[12]

Hyram Tyree, who in his early life worked as a shoemaker and elevator boy, would later serve Chattanooga's African American community as an alderman of the bustling 4th Ward.

Tyree settled in Chattanooga at the age of twenty, and went to work in such places as the Knoxville and Kentucky Railroad and the Abbott & Goldsmith brickyard. Although he lost his right leg during the time he worked as a coupler at the Western & Atlantic Railroad, Tyree was too much of a progressive thinker to let such a challenge handicap him. He eventually became chairman of the Republican Executive Committee, and in 1899, he was elected alderman of the fourth ward. He was no token alderman, either; he reportedly "brought improvements to his ward, dispensed minor posts, and served on special committees on the board." One of those committees investigated favoritism in the conduct of the police department.[13]

Aside from his alderman position, Tyree also served as school commissioner for ten years. He was a tireless worker who was known as "a race man who never lost an opportunity to aid in [his race's] development."[14] This philosophy apparently carried over into his personal life too, because one of his sons, Wesley Tyree, served as deputy sheriff of Hamilton County, and another son, William, served as a mail carrier.

Of course, the list of early Chattanooga African Americans could go on. Needless to say, these same African Americans who as Civil War soldiers had helped build Chattanooga's National Cemetery, Chattanooga's Water Works and even the M.C. Meigs Bridge were now free to start and manage their own businesses. They did just that, and they did it very successfully.

The Coming of the Steele Orphanage

In 1882, the entire population of Chattanooga fell into the deadly hands of a smallpox epidemic. The mere fact that an alarming number of lives—both black and white—were lost as a result of the epidemic meant that it was most probably the *Variola major* strain of smallpox that swung the death blade throughout the city. *V. major* typically took twenty to forty percent of those persons unfortunate enough to fall into its clutches, and it showed in the African American community of Chattanooga in 1883 and 1884.

The Chattanooga African American community might be newly freed and ready to pursue their own interests, but they soon discovered that there were many other variables besides slavery that could hinder their progress. In this case, they found themselves basically discarded with no real medical recourse for their ailments other than to remain at home and suffer in silence and isolation. They had Dr. Thomas William Haigler, who had settled in Chattanooga in 1878, but he was only one physician among hundreds of ailing patients. Many of the more seriously ill African Americans were hastily sent to "the county poor house, east of town near the river,"[15] which at that time was the closest thing the city had to a hospital facility. Other than that, they were forced to lie at home and wait for the disease to run its course…or to kill them.

The disease took an alarming number of victims. In a July 3, 1883, *Chattanooga Times* article, one city judge discussed the devastation that the disease brought upon the African American community.

> *The ravages of small pox has* [sic] *left an amount of poverty and destitution among the colored population that is truly alarming. I have in my hands the names of 368 colored children in this city under twelve years of age that are orphaned and the most of them paupers. What to do with all these unfortunate children is more than I can suggest. We must attend to them…Unless there is a change in their training and education, the jails, work house and penitentiary will be too small to accommodate them.*

But before anything could be done, the merciless smallpox epidemic hit again. The winter of late 1883 and the spring of 1884 resulted in an even more frightening barrage of African American deaths. The *Chattanooga Times* newspaper was chock-full of the names of Negro patients listed under the monthly mortuary column,[14] wiped out by such diseases as consumption, marasmus, chronic diarrhea, congestive chills, capillary bronchitis, dropsy and smallpox. And of course each adult death meant another homeless, penniless and absolutely friendless child in need of a guardian. Many of these friendless urchins ended up scavenging on the streets. Before long, their desperate attempt to stay alive was interpreted as criminal activity, and they were soon consigned to the chain gangs, doomed to a life of hard labor.

A few years later, a *Chattanooga Times* article dated May 5, 1886, described the epidemic of 1883–84:

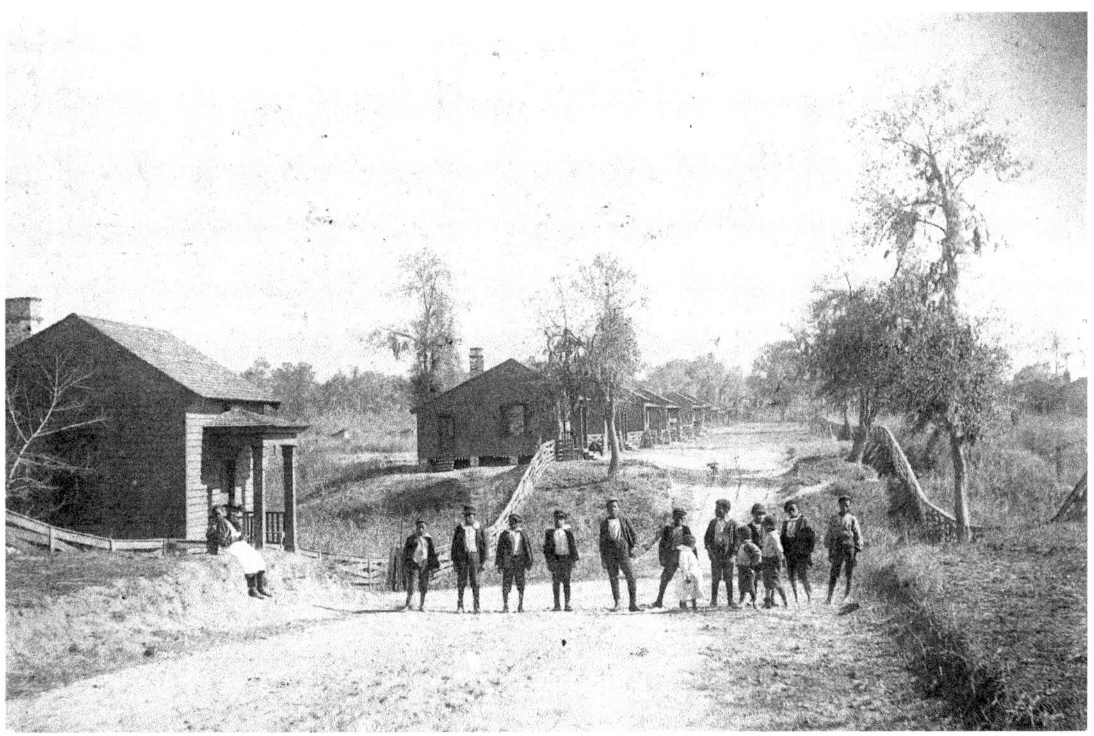

This is a photograph of the original frame houses for the Steele Orphanage for Colored Children. The orphanage was founded in 1884 by Almira Steele, but arsonists burned the houses down in 1885. There are fifteen unidentified African American children in this photograph. *Photograph courtesy of E.Y. Chapin, Walter Cline and Frank Stoops of the Chattanooga Half Century Club.*

> *For white orphan children and children of those unfit or incapable of taking charge of them, a provision has been made by the efforts of a few noble women of Chattanooga, aided by the contributions of the benevolent of the town and supplemented by the assistance of the county of Hamilton. But for the colored orphan children in like condition, no provision of any kind had been made. What was to become of all these children, who had bodies to be fed and clothed, minds to be trained, and souls to be saved?*

Into this downward spiral of death and despair came Almira Steele, a white woman born near Chelsea, Massachusetts. Steele was in search of missionary work, and came south to loan her services to anyone in need of assistance. She believed that everyone—African Americans included—deserved a chance. She found work—more than she bargained for, as a matter of fact—in the African American community of Chattanooga, Tennessee. The moment she crossed into the city limits, Steele felt the sheer desperation of the people and immediately set about aiding the waifs that no one cared for.

Steele invested all her own personal funds of $2,000—a small fortune in those days, and founded the Steele Orphanage for Needy Children, known synonymously as the Colored Orphan's Home. She set up individual huts and designated them male and female dormitories. These dormitories were located in the 800 block of Ford Street near Palmetto—a location that would, 120 years later, be known as the University of

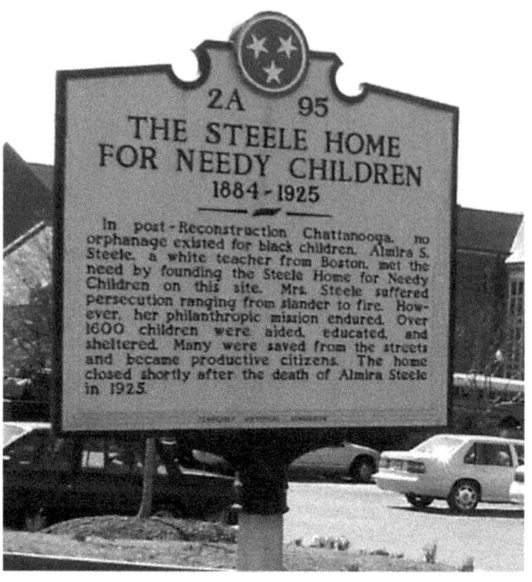

This photograph shows the historical marker for the Steele Orphanage. The University of Tennessee campus can be seen in the background. *Photograph courtesy of Rita Lorraine Hubbard, March 2005.*

Tennessee at Chattanooga. Steele opened the doors of the Steele Orphanage for Needy Children on April 24, 1884.[17]

The orphanage hastily began its mission work by servicing three of the city's most desperate African American children, the youngest of which was a baby girl of one week and the oldest a boy of fourteen rescued from the local chain gang. The boy was said to be the son of "one of the worthiest and most industrious colored men of Chattanooga, who had perished in the yellow fever epidemic of 1878."[18] After the death of his parents, he had lived on the streets for years, foraging for food and scraping by until some wayward activity or other had been interpreted as criminal activity and he had been consigned to a chain gang.[19] But with the shelter of the Steele Orphanage and the tender guidance of Almira Steele, the fourteen-year-old was rescued from his fate and was eventually sent to Northfield, Massachusetts, to attend school.

More children were quickly added to the roster, until a total of 133 destitute children were being serviced. Of these, eleven would eventually die of various diseases, including consumption, measles and cholera, but the remainder would cling to life under Almira's loving hands. The task was hard; in fact, it was almost impossible, especially when arsonists expressed their unhappiness over what they may have felt was too much interest in the Negro race and torched Steele's precious Steele Orphanage dormitories in November 1885. Yet Steele refused to throw in the towel. She simply went to her friends and colleagues and raised money to construct a new $18,000 brick building that would accommodate the growing number of orphans.

Over three thousand African Americans and a number of whites gathered to lay the cornerstone for the new Steele Orphanage. Once it began operation again, Steele pressed ever forward, bravely accepting sole responsibility for paying employee wages and for providing lights, fuel, furniture, bedding and clothing for all the children she served.

Of course, the African American community did not simply sit idly by while she worked for the orphans of their race. The Loomis and Hart Manufacturing Company, located at 719 East 9th Street, employed a large number of African American men. A group of these men were known to donate a portion of their desperately needed salary—usually twenty-five cents each—toward the upkeep and feeding of the Steele Orphanage children.[20]

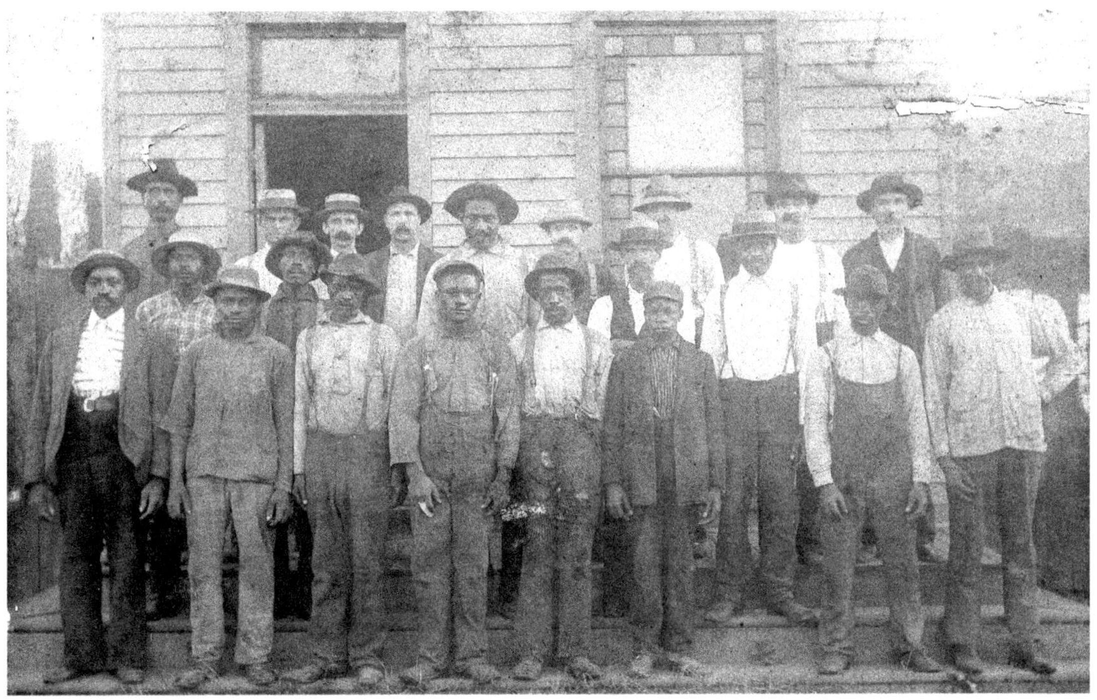

A large group of African American workers standing in front of the Loomis and Hart Manufacturing Company, located at 719 East 9th Street. These men were known to donate a portion of their salary (usually twenty-five cents) toward the upkeep and feeding of the Steele Orphanage children. *Photograph courtesy of the Paul A. Heiner Collection, ©1897.*

But what the African American community couldn't provide, Steele acquired on her own. She never tired, continuing to aid the medically, emotionally, physically and financially needy children while she waited for someone to come along who could change the face of medical care for the entire African American community…for only a change in medical care would change the orphan problem.

That change would of course come many years later when Dr. Emma Rochelle Wheeler built Walden Hospital, Chattanooga's first and only African American teaching hospital.

A Diverse Population

Chattanooga's African American community was diverse. First, they were composed of former slaves who escaped from other cities and plantations and made their way to the Federal forces in Chattanooga. They were also composed of the refugees and drifters who followed the Federal soldiers from city to city as they conquered portions of the South. The largest majority of these refugees, drifters and ex-slaves remained in Chattanooga after the Civil War and became citizens.

These African American citizens quickly moved into the workforce after the war. They were mail carriers, foremen, pharmacists, coal dealers and undertakers.

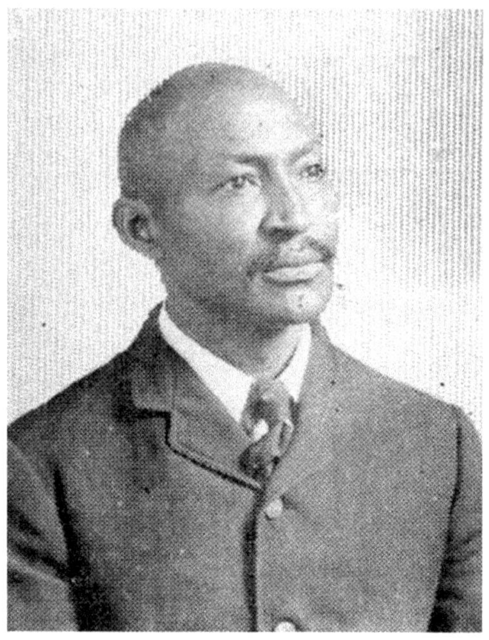

Mr. L.C. Gibbs, one of the wealthiest and most well-known contractors in Chattanooga, Tennessee. *Photograph courtesy of* 1904 Biography and Achievements of the Colored Citizens of Chattanooga *by J. Bliss White.*

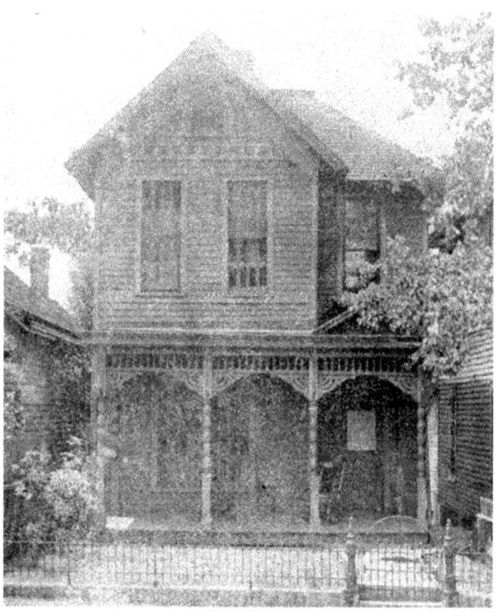

This is a photograph of the home of L.C. Gibbs. At one time only the very wealthy African American could afford a two-story structure like this one. *Photograph courtesy of* 1904 Biography and Achievements of the Colored Citizens of Chattanooga *by J. Bliss White.*

They were also employed at such places as Chattanooga Plow Company, Southern Railroad, Ross-Mehan Foundry, U.S. Cast Iron & Pipe Foundry and the Empire Steam Laundry.

But there were more prominent African Americans too, like Professor James A. Henry, Chattanooga's first Negro school principal, and the Reverend Joseph E. Smith, a well-known minister and civic leader. There was the ever popular L.C. Gibbs, one of the wealthiest contractors—Negro or white—in all of Hamilton County, who became a contractor at the tender age of eighteen, and who became one of the most successful businessmen in all of Hamilton County. Gibbs accumulated much valuable real estate in various sections of the city. His home was a far cry from the typical African American home at the turn of the century.

The dynamic Noah Walter Parden was another prominent member of the Chattanooga African American community. Parden, an attorney, was often referred to by whites as a "trouble-maker and community agitator" because he fought so vigorously for his clients. He often cited chapters from Psalms and Proverbs when he addressed the juries. Parden would go on to become the first African American ever to win a stay of execution for his Negro client from the Supreme Court; and the first Negro designated as lead attorney in a Supreme Court case.[21]

There was D.T. Edinburg, a Negro contractor who had just been elected to a four-year term as school commissioner at large, and who had accumulated an extensive amount of property in Chattanooga. There was Robert Jenkins Stanford, street foreman for the Lookout Water Company—forerunner of the Tennessee-American Water Company—who was in full charge of all street work, including putting down new mains and making repairs.[22]

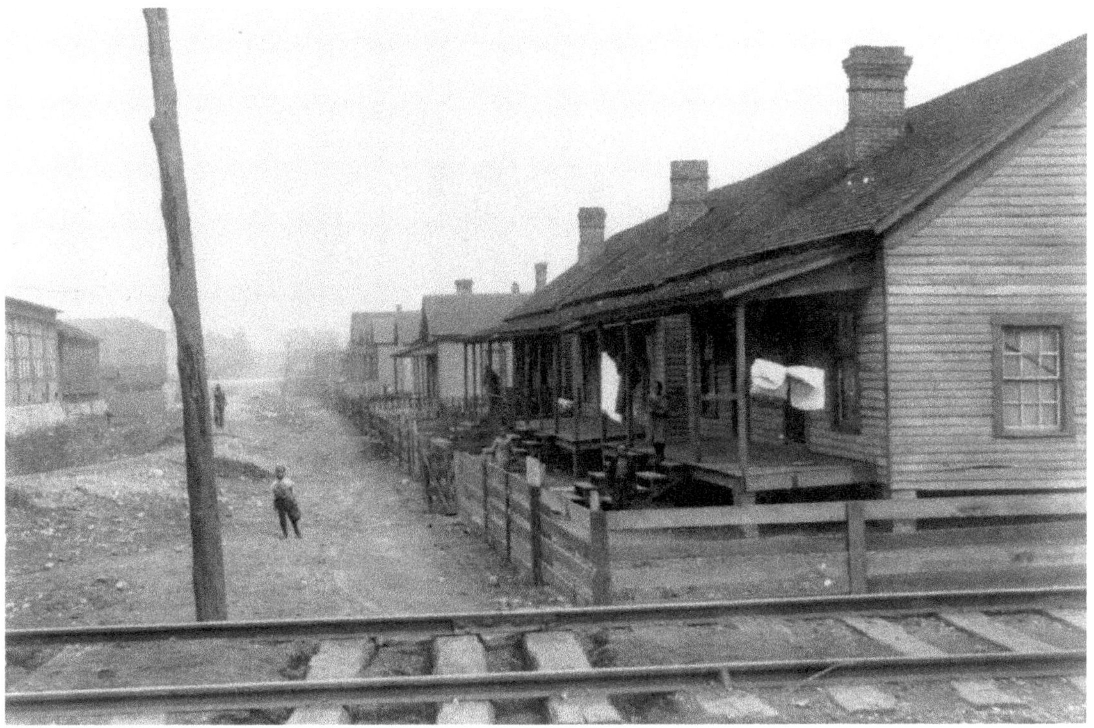

A Glance into Chattanooga's Past: This 1899 photograph was titled "Negro Homes; Homes of the Poorer Class." The photograph was part of a group of photographs displayed in the American Negro Exhibit at the Paris exposition in 1900. *Photograph courtesy of the Library of Congress Prints and Photographs Division, ©1899.*

There was the well-known John Drain, a barber of eighteen years, who was credited with establishing Chattanooga's system of city hack stands, and there was the wealthy John G. Higgins, another barber, who owned eleven prominent barber shops and who was the inventor of the wildly successful Eureka Straightening Comb. John G. Higgins's granddaughter, Josephine Dorsey, would eventually marry Dr. Emma R. Wheeler's nephew and adopted son, George, and set up housekeeping in New York.[23]

There was prominent Negro citizen J. Bliss White, the author who boldly penned Chattanooga's Negro history, *Biography and Achievements of the Colored Citizens of Chattanooga*. Bliss was also a librarian, an orator and a lawyer, often practicing with his attorney father, J.W. White. The senior White had had his own illustrious career and had been a lawyer, a teacher, a justice of the peace, an alderman, a tax assessor and a poor commissioner. He had even headed Chattanooga's short-lived PennySavings Bank for Negroes.[24]

There was the irrepressible Randolph Miller, the outspoken ex-slave who fought with Sherman's army during his famous march to the sea, and who had now turned fearless editor of his own creation—*The Blade*—a newspaper so fiery and outspoken, it was quoted all across the United States in the form of short quips called "Gems From *The Blade*." Like an early prototype for the civil rights leaders of the later years, Miller spoke his whole mind without hesitation.

In July 1905 Miller flamboyantly organized a boycott in which he denounced the oppressive Jim Crow laws in Chattanooga that governed those who rode the

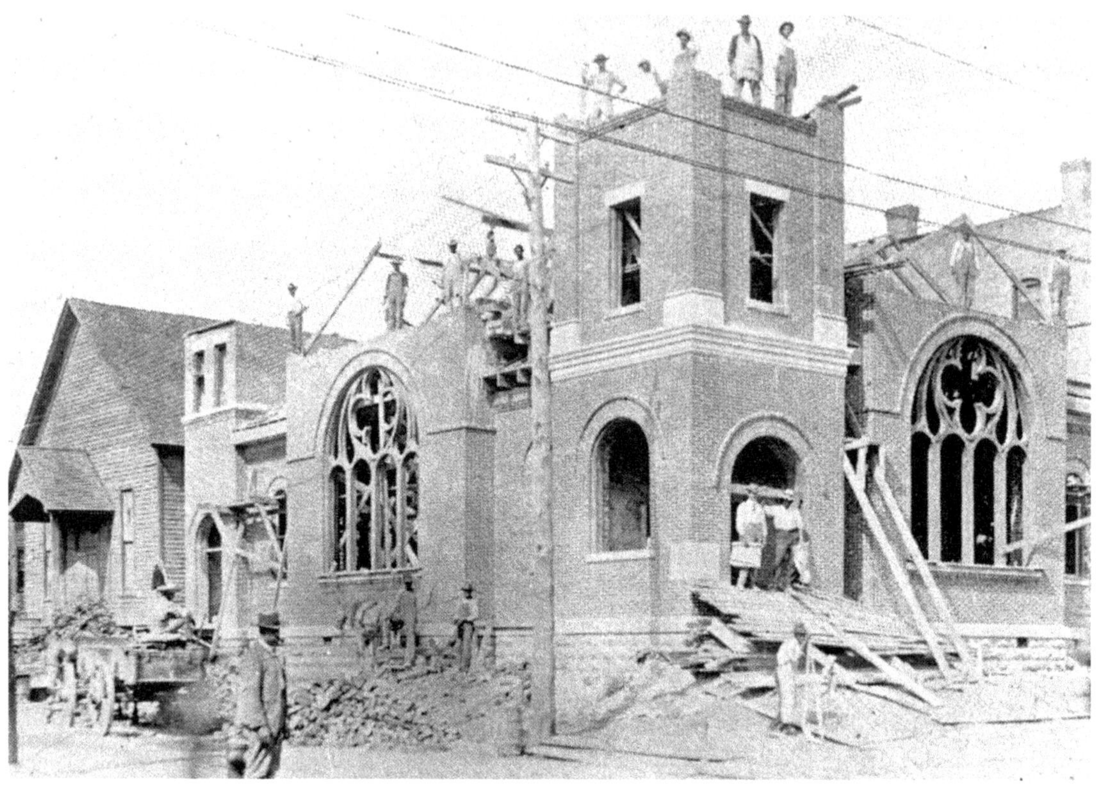

This is a photograph of the First Congregational Church, under construction in 1904. It was located at the corner of 9th Street and A Street (Lindsay Street). The church was built using African American labor provided by Alston & Johnson contractors. *Photograph courtesy of* 1904 Biography and Achievements of the Colored Citizens of Chattanooga *by J. Bliss White.*

public streetcars. In a bold move, Miller started a hack line—a taxi service using horse-and-buggy—in an attempt to accommodate Negro riders who, after their fare was taken, were treated with utter disrespect on the public streetcars.

And of course, there was the dashing young George Washington Franklin Jr., personal friend to Booker T. Washington and one of Chattanooga's most successful and wealthy businessmen. Franklin owned a blacksmith business, his own hack line and a prosperous wood and coal yard. He also owned and operated both the East View and the Pleasant Garden cemeteries,[25] and provided an accompanying undertaking business—which he also owned—that was the forerunner of the Franklin-Strictland funeral home. With his elegant hearse and his beautiful team of horses, Franklin furnished coffins, caskets and robes of all grades and all prices. His undertaking business is still in existence over one hundred years later, and still carries his prominent surname.

The fact was, Chattanooga's African American community was extremely active and was known to draw visitors from all over the South. After all, Chattanooga was the home of the Martin Hotel, the largest African American hotel in the South, and that same hotel that welcomed such greats as Cab Calloway, Lena Horne, The Ink Spots, Fats Domino and Mahalia Jackson, to name a few. Chattanooga was also the

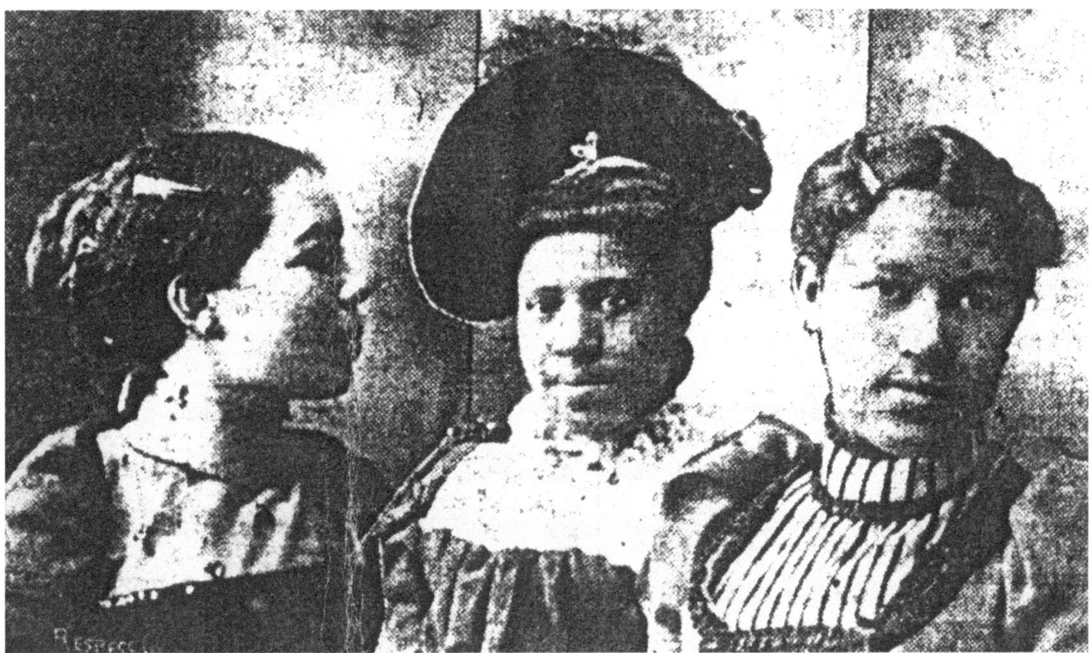

An 1899 photograph of Howard High School graduates Addie Streeter, Mary E. Hawkins and Pearl R. Whiteside. *Photograph courtesy of the* Daily Times.

home of the Haslerig Dairy—predecessor of Happy Valley Farms—and the only Negro-owned dairy farm of its type in the South.

It was the home of Dr. O.L. Davis, hailed as the South's first African American female dentist. It was the home of Lincoln Park, which opened in 1938 and had the first lighted softball fields for African Americans in the entire Southeast and the finest pool for Negroes anywhere.[26] It was even situated right on the border of the Chickamauga Battlefield, where old Uncle Mark Thrash, the internationally-known ex-slave and ex-Civil War soldier who would live to be almost 123, entertained visitors from all over the United States and told them about his thrilling Civil War escapades.

All of these people and places drew visitors—African American and white, to the Chattanooga area. Even Walden Hospital—the only Negro Hospital for miles in any direction—drew an unknown number of visitors, both healthy and sick, into the city.

2.

Early African American Schools

This section offers a brief description of two early African American schools in Chattanooga. It also includes photographs of early schools in different sections of Hamilton County. Of course, this is not an exhaustive list.

Howard School

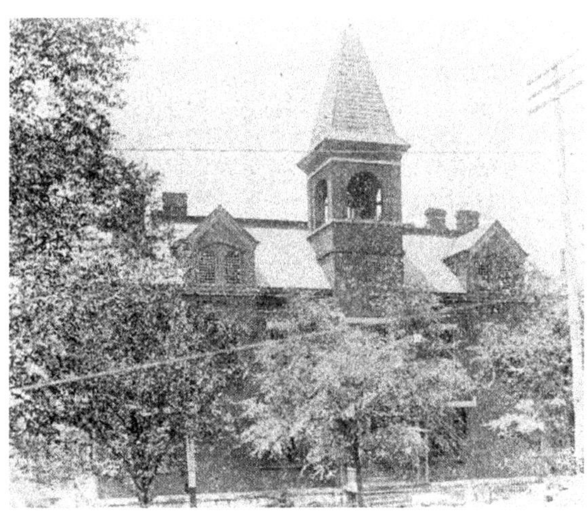

This is a photograph of Howard Free School when it was located at 7th and Pine Streets. *Photograph courtesy of* 1904 Biography and Achievements of the Colored Citizens of Chattanooga *by J. Bliss White.*

Chattanooga African Americans were definitely at the forefront when it came to educating their own. Howard Free School, the first school in Chattanooga for African Americans, was actually the first public school—black or white—in the entire city of Chattanooga. While white citizens were still in the midst of lively discussions about opening public schools for their own children, classes had already begun at Howard Free School in September 1872.[27]

Although Howard's beginnings are sketchy at times, a detailed account of the school was documented in an 1886 essay by young Ella B. Harris. Harris was an African American youth preparing for graduation from the fledgling school system; in fact, Harris was third in line on the graduation roster. Bell Washington would be the first to graduate in 1886, Augustus Wickliff would graduate the following year in 1887, and Harris would follow in 1888.

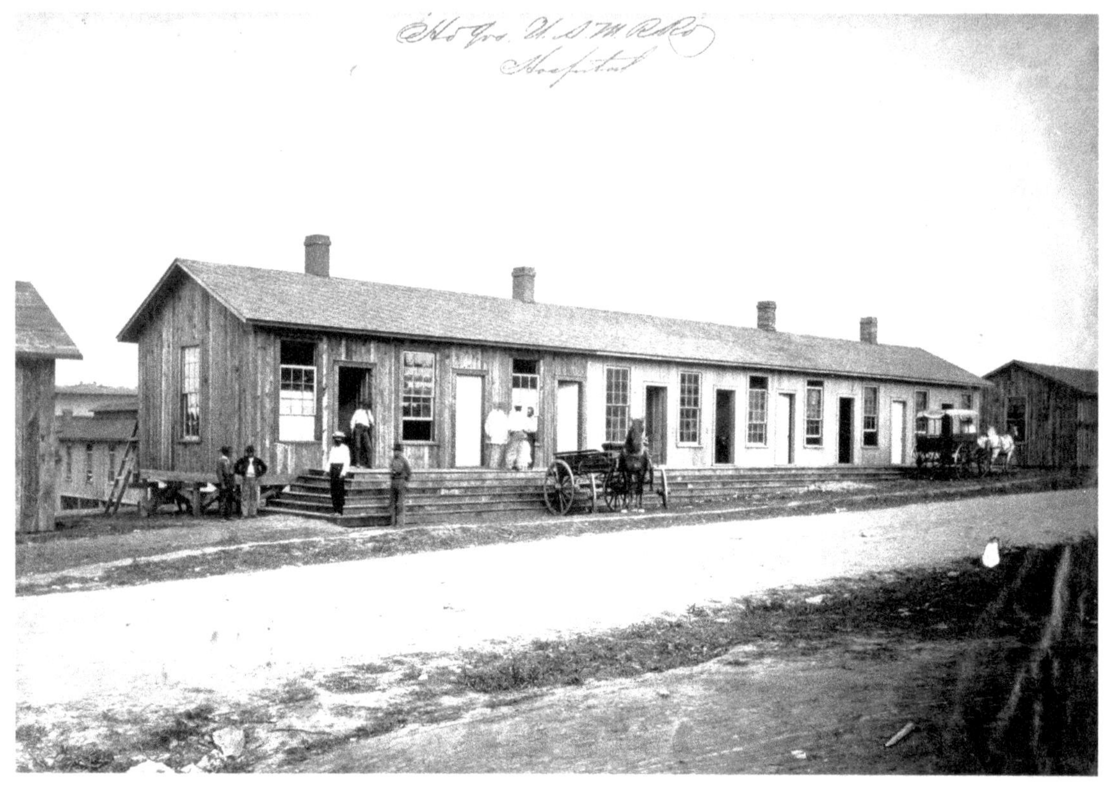

According to an 1886 essay written by Howard High School freshman Ella D. Harris, Howard School began in one of several old-fashioned, time-scarred buildings on Chestnut Street like this one, which had been used as a hospital barracks during the Civil War. *Reproduction of National Archives photograph no. 165-C-1046, provided by Chattanooga-Hamilton County Bicentennial Library.*

In this documentation of Howard's early history, Harris was the primary speaker during Bell Washington's graduation ceremony. According to Harris's essay, Howard School began in approximately 1865, in one of several old-fashioned, time-scarred buildings on Chestnut Street that had once been used as hospital barracks during the Civil War. (See photo for an example of the type of early building in which Howard Free School classes were held.)

Of course, Ewing Ogden Tade (also known as E.O. Tade) was largely responsible for starting Howard School. He sent for teachers from the North, and one of them was a man by the name of Mr. Fernel.

According to Harris's essay, Mr. Fernel conducted the first school for "coloreds" that had ever been organized in the city of Chattanooga. She claimed that Fernel did not have an easy time, and that the majority of the Southerners looked upon him with what she described as "the bitterest scorn." But according to Harris, Fernel was indifferent to this scorn and was successful in his endeavors.

Harris went on to describe Fernel as a man who "put the wheel of knowledge in operation so that his work would always go forward and never turn backward." Afterward, the work was again taken up by Tade, who was also a clerk at the

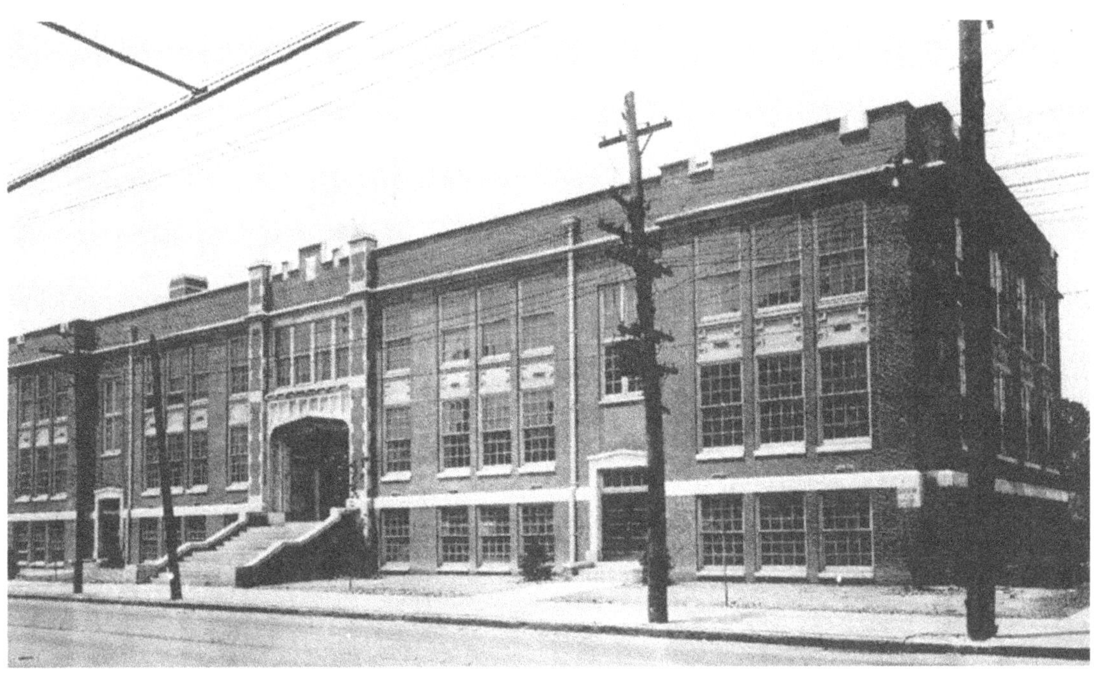

A pre-1954 shot of old Howard School, located on 10th and Carter Streets. *Photograph courtesy of* Buildings by Wilson Since 1912, *©1941 by George S. Myers Associated.*

Freedman's Savings Bank. Under Tade's supervision, the "Band of Hope" came into existence in or around 1867, and brought forth the city's best African American teachers.

Tade's wife, Mrs. E.O. Tade, worked closely with him, and soon the Howard School house was built on 9th Street.

Following is an excerpt from Ella B. Harris's 1886 essay. In it, she describes Howard schoolteachers as they were seen by both the African American and white community.

> *No school of the South has had a better corps of teachers from its foundation up to now, than Chattanooga...They long ago cast their bread upon the waters, and, should they return to Chattanooga now, they would find the grand result of their work. Instead of the white face alone instructing as of yore, they will be amazed to see ten or twelve from our race teaching, and most wonderful of all, a colored principal. Twenty years ago, the cloud of ignorance hung heavy and dark, but today what a beautiful contrast. We judge by the rapid strides taken in the past score of years that the twentieth century will bring about a most wonderful change...We who are young should be proud that we live at such a time when harmony, peace, friendship and love are no longer enemies in the south. All this has been brought about by the hand of providence by which we will always be led to a glorious success if we be but faithful to our every duty.*[28]

Howard School has had several locations, and the passage of time has clouded their chronology. However, it is known that the school was started in a church that

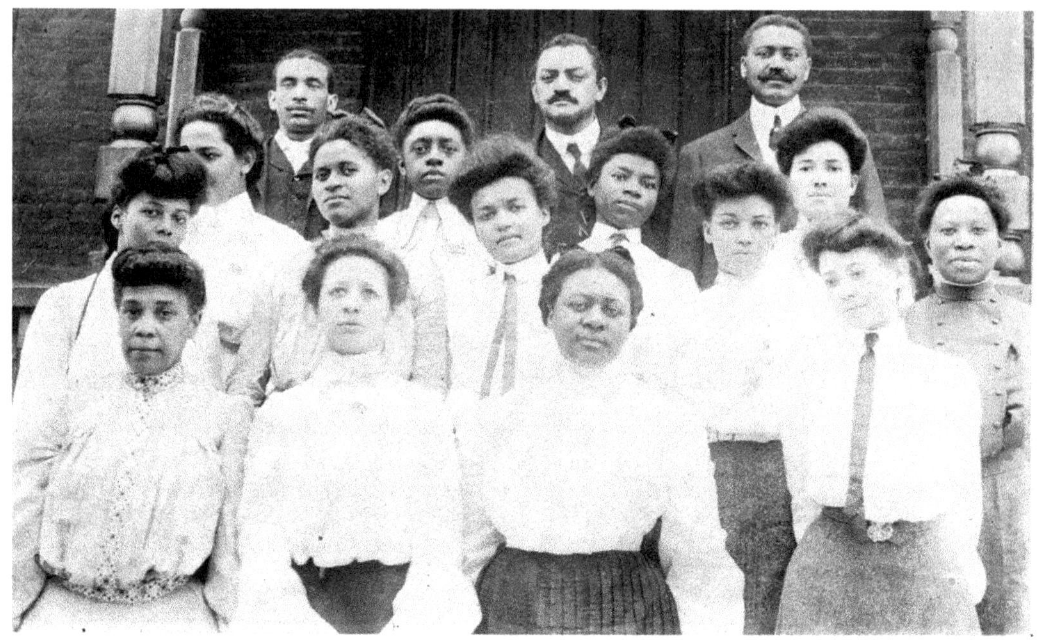

This is a 1904 photograph of a group of Howard School classroom teachers. Howard School was named in honor of General O.O. Howard, commissioner of the Freedman's Bureau. *Photograph courtesy of* 1904 Biography and Achievements of the Colored Citizens of Chattanooga *by J. Bliss White.*

was probably located at 7th and Pine Streets. By 1872, the school was incorporated into the city system. Again, the African American education system was innovative in Chattanooga. According to Charles D. McGuffey's *Standard History of Chattanooga*, while whites were just entering talks about starting a school for their children, Howard Free School was already in operation as of September 1872.

Howard School was named in honor of General O.O. Howard, commissioner of the Freedman's Bureau. According to some accounts, he was responsible for the pre-integration education of African Americans in Chattanooga, Tennessee.

Ella D. Harris
Third Chattanooga African American High School Graduate

Ella D. Harris was the third African American to graduate from Howard High School in Chattanooga, Tennessee. Her graduation day was May 26, 1888, and she was the sole graduate that year.

The ceremony was held at the densely-packed First Congregational Church. Captain H.S. Chamberlain, president of the school board, was unable to attend Ella's graduation, so Adolph Ochs, owner of the *Chattanooga Times* newspaper, presented the diploma in his absence.

Ella's graduation essay was titled "Silent Influences." Unfortunately, no copy of the essay survives.

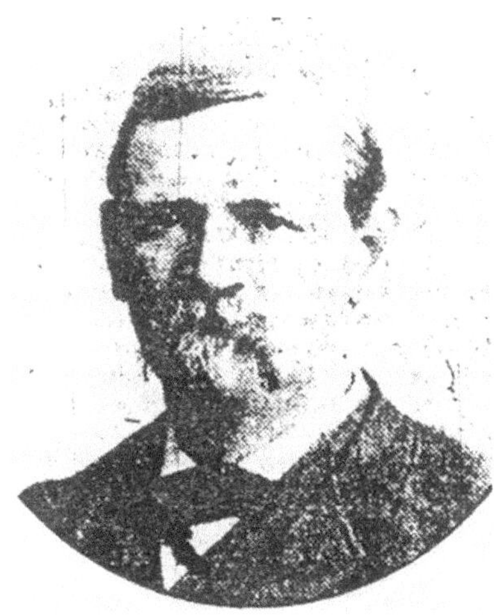

Professor L.B. Searle

Professor L.B. Searle was one of Chattanooga's early African American teachers. Searle was also principal of Howard School in 1878.

Bell Washington First African American High School Graduate

On a Friday afternoon, inside a packed house and amidst showers of verbal praise and fanfare, Miss Bell G. Washington became the first African American—male or female—to graduate from high school in Chattanooga, Tennessee. The occasion was so singular that Bell was "completely surrounded with bouquets of flowers" when she arose to receive her diploma.

It was May 21, 1886, and this was Howard School's very first graduation exercise. Young Washington wore a beautiful graduation gown and held tightly to her prized diploma. She had started school at the age of nine, and now at age nineteen she had finally reached her goal.

The ceremony marked a joyous occasion for Chattanooga's African American community. These African Americans had only been free from the shackles of slavery for twenty-one years at the time Washington graduated, and this day served to foreshadow the glorious years to come when every African American child in the community would have the opportunity to graduate from formal schooling.

The ceremony was held at the First Congregational Church, which was located on Lindsay and 9th Streets. As mentioned, Ella B. Harris was one of the speakers at Bell's graduation, and she delivered a wonderfully detailed account of Howard High School's history.

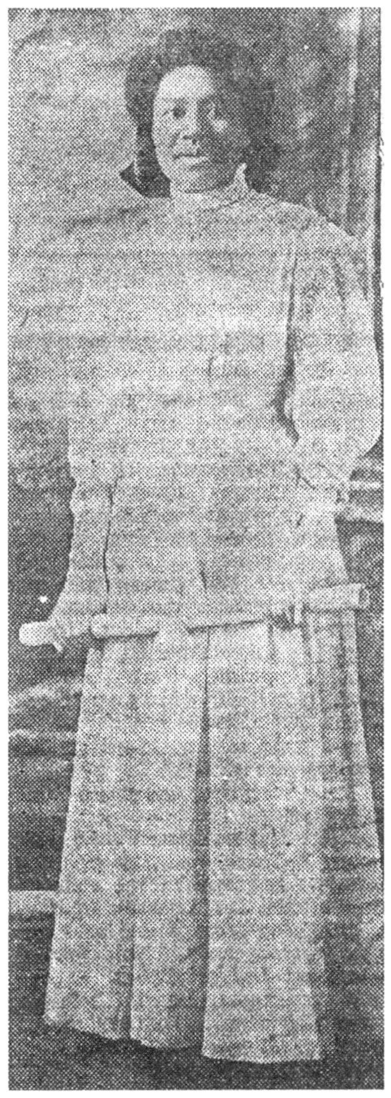

Top: An early photograph of Professor L.B. Searle, one of Chattanooga's early African American schoolteachers. Searle was also principal of the Howard Free School in 1878. *Photograph courtesy of the* Chattanooga Times, *July 1, 1928, Jubilee No. 25.*

Bottom: This beautiful lady is Bell Washington, who became Chattanooga's first African American high school graduate on May 21, 1886. Bell is wearing her graduation dress and holding her diploma in her hands. *Photograph courtesy of the* Chattanooga Daily Times, *September 18, 1938.*

Following her speech, Washington brought the ceremony to a close by reading her original essay, titled, "From School Life into Life's School." Unfortunately, no facsimile of the essay has survived; however, it was said to be "well written and delivered in an intelligent manner."[29] Captain H.S. Chamberlain, president of the school board, presented Bell's diploma.

Washington would go on to teach in Chattanooga city's school system for thirty-five years, finally asking for a voluntary retirement pension. At that time, she retired to her residence at 211 Pine Street.

Augustus Wickliff
First African American Male High School Graduate

African American male Augustus Wickliff, like Bell G. Washington a year before him, was the sole graduating senior in the class of 1887. He received his diploma before a packed, jubilant house, and he too was surrounded by scores of flowers and floral tributes.

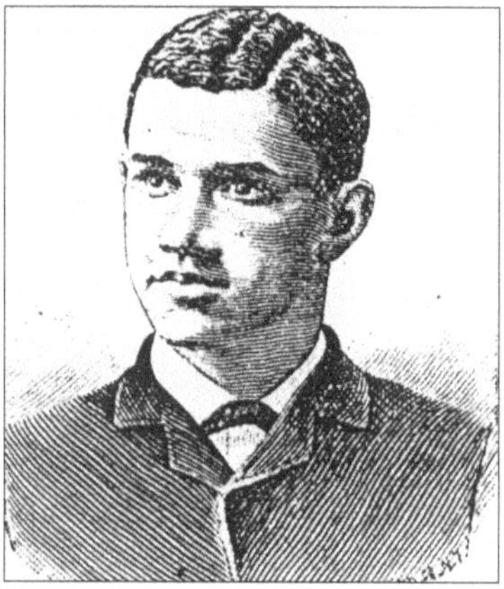

But Wickliff's graduation was very different from Washington's. This was because he was the first African American male ever to graduate from a high school in Chattanooga, Tennessee.

A May 21, 1887 sketch of Augustus Wickliffe, Chattanooga's second African American high school graduate, and its very first African American male graduate. *Photograph courtesy of the* Chattanooga Daily Times.

Captain H.S. Chamberlain, president of the school board, presented Wickliff's diploma, but he did not stop there. He could not pass up the opportunity to speak at such a momentous occasion. He bestowed upon Wickliff and the jubilant audience a momentous speech fit for the occasion. The following excerpt is taken directly from the Howard School 1887 Graduation Exercises:

> *Augustus, I am glad to present you this diploma tonight. You may be called the pioneer boy graduate of the Howard Schools. A young lady* [Bell] *graduated a year ago, but you are the first young* [African American] *man that has ever been accorded that honor. I have performed no duty today that is more pleasant than the one I am about to perform. Even the presentation of diplomas to a large class of graduates today did not afford me more joy than the presentation of this one diploma. It shows that the colored people are making progress. We sometimes think they are moving slowly, but then it is surely. One thing our colored friends want to do, and that is help the schools by sending their children to school promptly and doing everything they can to build them up. The colored race is already taking its place in many of the trades here in the South. It has only begun in the march of progress. The colored people must be educated. The first young man has graduated tonight. That is a start, and a good one. Augustus, in [sic] behalf of the school board of the city of Chattanooga, I present you this diploma, with the hope that you may meet with great prosperity.*[30]

Needless to say, those African Americans who filled the church to bursting in order to see the very first Negro male in Chattanooga receive his diploma responded with a long round of applause. Professor James A. Henry, a well-known and much loved figure in African American history, gave Augustus his blessing as he marched across the stage.

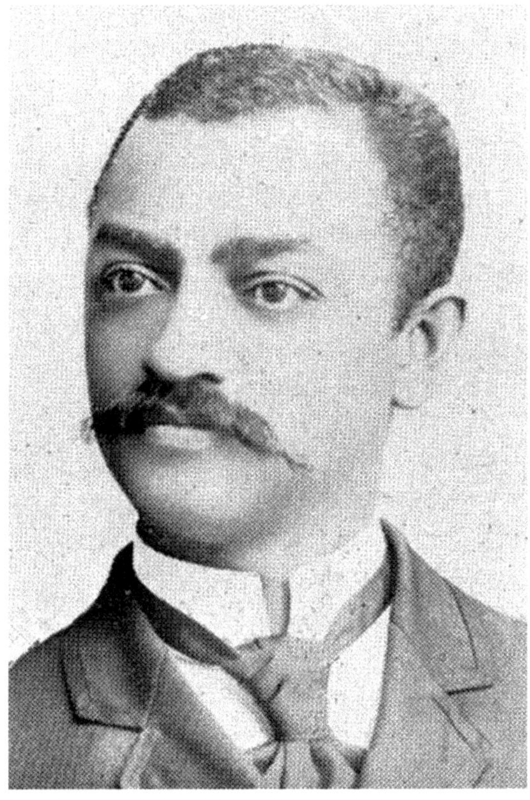

An early 1900 photograph of Professor James A. Henry, the first African American principal in Chattanooga City Schools. Professor Henry was present at the landmark graduations of Bell Washington and Augustus Wickliffe, the first African American female and male graduate of Howard High School, respectively. Professor Henry became grand master of the Chattanooga Masons in the early 1900s. *Photograph courtesy of* 1904 Biography and Achievements of the Colored Citizens of Chattanooga *by J. Bliss White.*

Professor James A. Henry

Professor James A. Henry was the first African American principal in Chattanooga City Schools. He attended the landmark graduation of Bell Washington in 1886, and he was given much of the credit when Augustus Wickliff, Chattanooga's first African American male, graduated from high school in 1887.

On Wickliff's graduation day, a *Chattanooga Times* reporter showered Professor Henry with more praise than he gave the graduating senior:

> *To Professor Henry is due much of the credit for the thorough and careful presentation that had been made by a lot of the performers* [at Augustus Wickliff's graduation]. *There was no hitch or delay but everything moved off sprightly and in the most perfect order. Several persons present from a distance said the Howard School commencement was the most successful colored school commencement they had ever attended and reflected great credit upon the race in this city.*[31]

Professor Henry was born in Buffalo, New York, in 1859, and received his education in Buffalo schools. He received a BA degree from Atlanta University in 1883, and immediately located to Chattanooga as an assistant teacher in Howard High School at its then Georgia Avenue location. He served as an assistant, until he succeeded J.S. Fowler as principal. During his thirty-one years of service with Chattanooga public schools, Professor Henry was recognized "not only in Chattanooga and Tennessee as one of the foremost colored educators, but his ability was recognized throughout the south."[32]

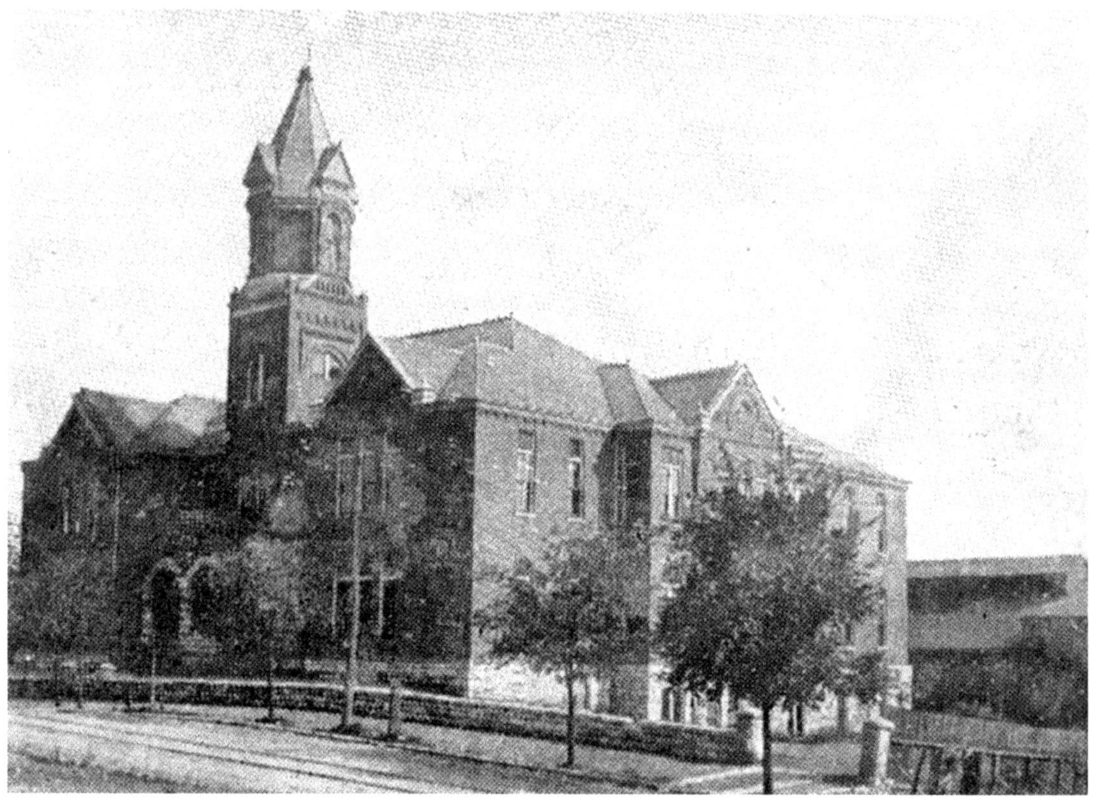

This is an early photograph of the original Montgomery Avenue School. Today Montgomery Avenue is known as Main Street. *Photograph courtesy of* 1904 Biography and Achievements of the Colored Citizens of Chattanooga *by J. Bliss White.*

MONTGOMERY AVENUE SCHOOL

Prior to the year 1881, it was the practice of the city of Chattanooga to use white teachers to teach African American children. But in 1881, city officials decided to conduct what they termed "an experiment," and made the move to use African American teachers to teach African American children.

Professor H.B. Wyatt, then superintendent of schools, appointed Mrs. Tena Grant-Gilmore to be one of the first African American teachers employed by the school system. Grant-Gilmore's classroom was located in a one-room box church called Mt. Paran, located on Whiteside (Broad) Street. She was assigned what the city described as "only a few students," but was actually close to thirty-five children in number. Later the church was relocated, and pupil enrollment grew to 150.

Once the church relocated and enrollment increased, a request was quickly made for more teachers. The city added two more African American women—Miss Susie Redding and Miss Mary Simington—to assist Grant-Gilmore. Children from the fourth and fifth ward attended this school, and Grant-Gilmore soon wrote out a petition for a larger building.

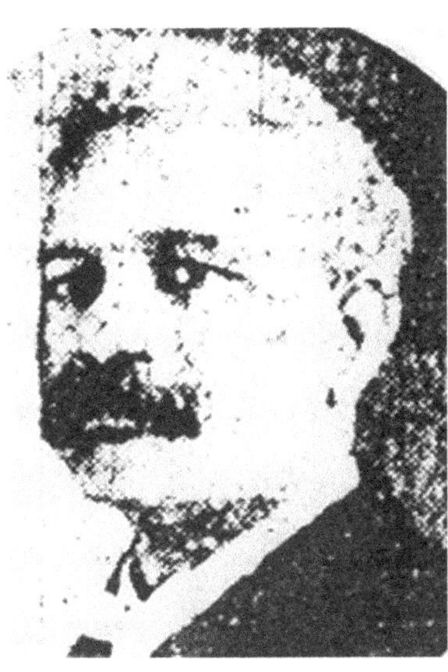

Rev. Joseph E. Smith

The Reverend Joseph E. Smith was appointed to select a suitable site for the growing "colored" school. Rev. Smith was pastor of the First Congregational Church, and was a member of the board of education. After careful consideration, Rev. Smith selected the Montgomery Avenue address.

Professor W.M. Singleton

Professor W.M. Singleton was named principal of the Montgomery Avenue School. His assistants were Mr. K. Lewis, Miss Sarah Grant, Miss Ida Bannister, Miss Carrie Bannister, Mrs. Washington Stypes, Miss Charity Coleman and Miss Tena Grant Gilmore.

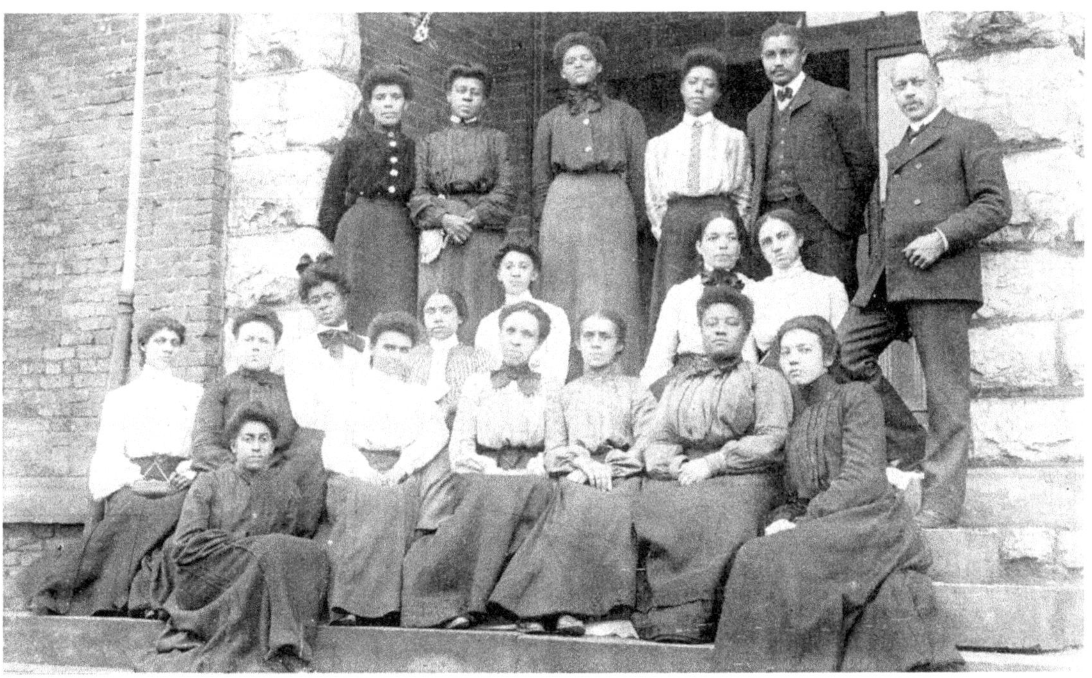

Top left: This is an early newspaper photograph of the Rev. Joseph E. Smith, who was pastor of the First Congregational Church and a member of the board of education in the late 1800s. Smith was appointed to select a suitable location for the growing "colored" school population, and he decided on the Montgomery Avenue address. *Photograph courtesy of the* Chattanooga Times, *July 1, 1928, Jubilee No. 25.*

Above: This is a 1904 photograph of the hardworking and industrious Montgomery Avenue schoolteachers. Professor W. M. Singleton, principal of the school, is standing on the far right. *Photograph courtesy of* 1904 Biography and Achievements of the Colored Citizens of Chattanooga *by J. Bliss White.*

OTHER EARLY AFRICAN AMERICAN SCHOOLS

Due to certain restrictions, many known early Chattanooga African American schools were not included in this volume. For example, the Gilmer Street Academy was once a bustling school for African American children who were eager to learn. Professor James A. Henry, one of the school's principal administrators in 1888, was assisted by an excellent staff of teachers, including J.W. White (father of J. Bliss White) and Robert C. Hawkins. Today Gilmer Street is known as East 8th Street.

In 1887 and 1888, the 9th Street School was in existence. Although the details of the school and its exact location are fuzzy, several of the African American teachers are identified. And of course, East 5th Street School was established in 1904, and served grades one through three.

All of these and other schools merit recognition; however, availability of early information and time and space constraints hindered their inclusion in this volume.

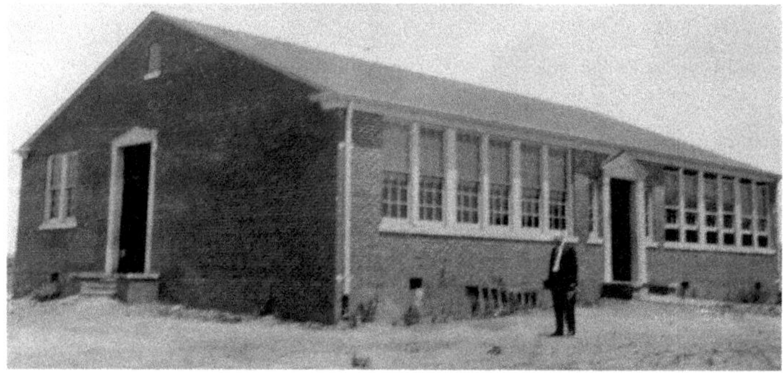

This is a June 1930 photograph of the Roland W. Hayes School (Colored) in Hamilton County. At one time, Flora I. Cox of Cross Street was principal. *Photograph courtesy of the Tennessee State Library and Archives.*

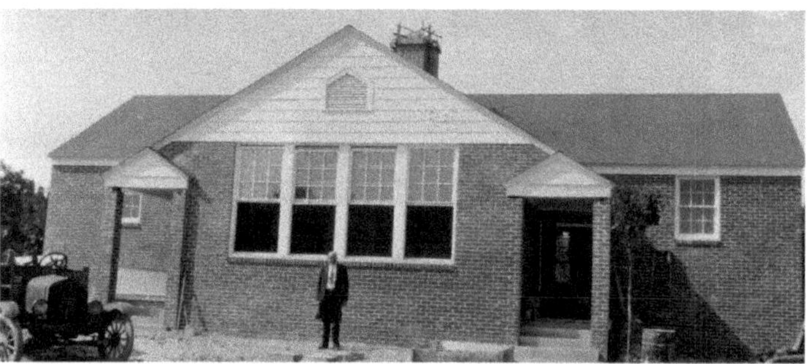

This is a June 1930 photograph of the Bakewell School (Colored) in Hamilton County. At one time, Leonard G. Robinson of Soddy, Tennessee, was principal. *Photograph courtesy of the Tennessee State Library and Archives.*

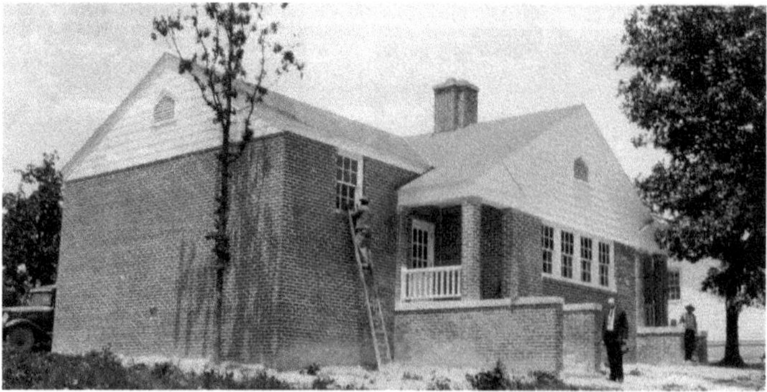

This is a June 1930 photograph of Booker T. Washington Colored School—also known as Washington High—in Hamilton County. At one time, Taz D. Upshaw Jr. of East 8th Street was principal. *Photograph courtesy of Tennessee State Library and Archives.*

Roll Call

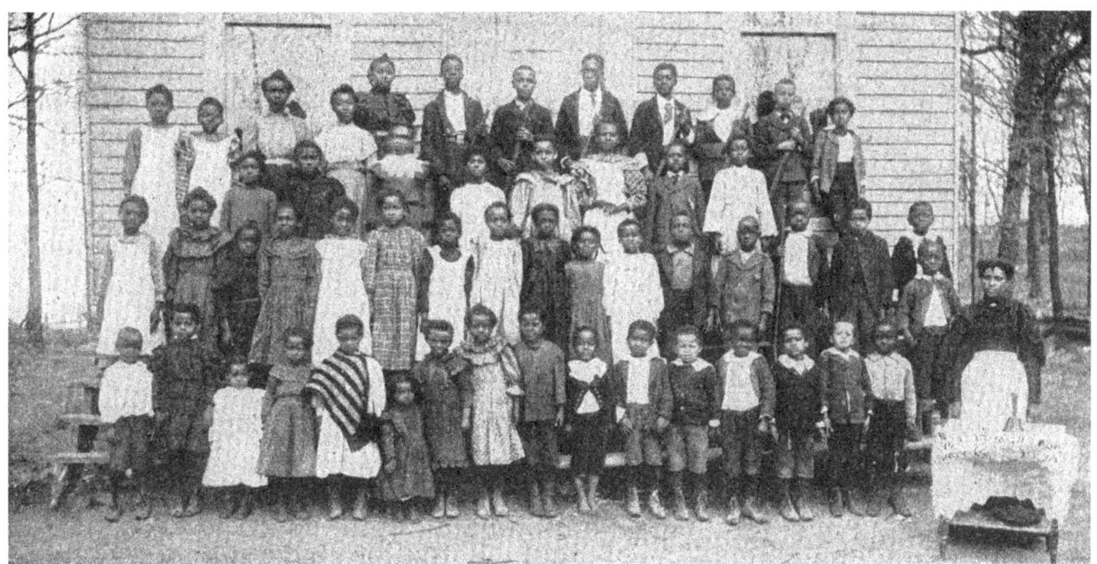

Gilmer Street School 1886 Roster

This is an 1892 photograph of the Bible and Sunshine Band of Chattanooga, Tennessee. At that time, Bible bands were created to teach women and children to read and understand the Bible. *Photograph courtesy of* In Christ's Stead: Autobiographical Sketches *by Joanna B. Moore.*

Room 1—W. F. Jackson, Teacher:
Charles Gooden, Lula Pace, John Battle, Ada Henderson, Nellie Battle, Isaiah Blake, Mary Whitaker, Addie Durroh, Addie Hoodenpyle, Samuel Heggie, Belle Calloway, Henrietta Mitchel, and E. Nickerson.Nellie Gooden, Jessie Lucas, Georgia Robinson, Lucy Edwards, Mrs. Lula Kemp, Augustus Wickliff, Azarine Taylor, E. Nickerson, G. Sewell, J. Sanders, W. Parden and Charles Henderson.
Fifth Grade—Room 2—W.H. Singleton, Teacher:
Alice Duncan, Henrietta Smith, Dicie Jordan, Mary Smith, Hattie Young, Walter Baxter, Louisa Moore, Nettie Brown, John Dunaway, Anna Shamlin, Lizzie Bezzids, James Glenn, Paralie Scruggs, Ada Keith, Carrie Johnson, Hattie Mays, Cora Calhoun, Maggie Cravens, Gracie Blaine, Ella McBride, Charles Carter, Annie Glass, Millie Sewell, N.B. Laurence, Ross Downs, Helen Hurd, Lena Alexander, Mamie Calloway, Nannie Armstrong, Annie Schooler, Walter Huston, Ida Vanburen and Martha Gaston.
Room 3—J.W. White, Teacher:[33]
William Brown, Walter Hodge, Thomas McConnell, Thomas Tillman, Lula Mitchell, George Armstrong, James McCannon, Lewis Cates, Hattie Greathouse, Mary Walker, Lillie Prince, Mary Tuncill, Callie Garner, Walter Stafford, Martha Prince, Mamie Harries, Francis Peters, Lula Wind, Martha Pierce, Estella Smith, Lillie Harlan, Alberta Lewis, Annie Crozier, Rosa Jordan, Della Elder, William Batts, Lula Rice, Bliss White,[34] Beatie McConnell, Eugenie Wallace, Charles Jackson, Eddie Gardner,

Camp Jacobs, Willie McKissick, Dora Fleming, Georgia Monroe, J. Mitchell, S. Pierson and Maggie Wells.

Room 4—R.C. Hawkins, Teacher:

Clarence Henderson, Ida Kenser, John Wommack, Mary Lee, Annie Winship, Mamie Jones, Kate Taylor, McHenry Landon, Sara Towers, Emma Osment, Rosa Thomason, Mabel Phillips, Laura McKissick, John Fralix, Annie Wooley, Lena Caldwell, Laura Huckless, Mattie Wooley and Carrie B. Waters.

Room 5—L.S.D. Sessions, Teacher:

Ellen Sanders, Annie Gay, Sarah Henderson, Lela Page, Anthony Prince, Lucy Dent, Robert Baxter, Mary Williams, Temple Irwin, Cora Carroll, Walter Protho, Charles Downs, Henry McIntyre, Charles McDermott, Frank Graham, James May, Willie Williams, Octavia Clark, Nellie Fields, Eddie Foster, Birdie Jacobs, Walter Irwing, Lula Nickerson, Benjamin Polk, Jennie Johnson, Quincy Irwin, Blanch Demorow, Arthur Calloway, Lizzie Underwood, Eliza Harper, Maggie Hamilton, Amanda Baxter, Josie Charlton, Ella Sanders, Lizzie Young, Anna Hurd, Vinnie Cob, Pearlie Smith, Sarah Scott, Thomas Jones, Joseph Rice, Ida Lee, Lucy Lewis, Etta Irving and Ida Wilburn.

Room 6—Miss L.C. Henderson, Teacher:

Moncello Fields, Lizzie Jones, Willie Vaughn, Mary Smith, Celia Henderson, Minnie Thomas, Charlie Vanburen, Ilena Brown, Ella Wildman and Willie Davis.

Room 7—Miss A.B. House, Teacher:

Cora Clements, Andrew Richardson, Sarah Gimar, Homer McCrary, Julia Howard, Walter Sommers, Mary Henderson, Cyrilla Hall, Joseph Battle, Mamie Farriss, Emmiel McCrary, Paulina Lampkins, Eddie Harlan, Mattie Farris and Maud Martin.

Room 8—Miss E.V. Alexander, Teacher:

Nathan Smith, Willie Blackwell, Cora McIntyre, Hannah Wooden, Millard Simpson, Solona Hill, Bertie Wooden, Emma Johnson, Oscar Rogers, Jessie Jackson and Jasper Woolly.

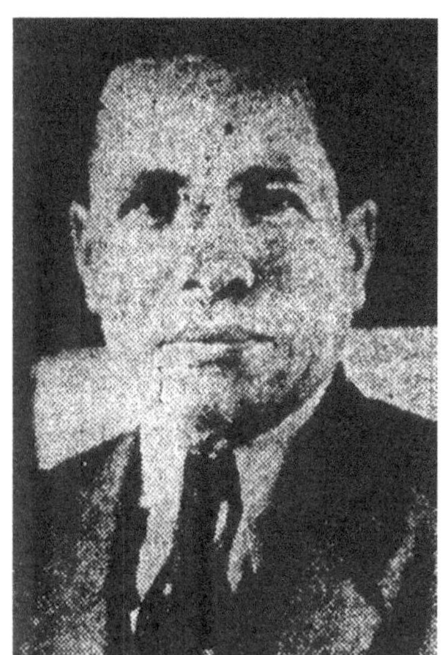

Howard School 1886 Roster

Room 1—J.S. Fowler, Teacher:

John Burgess, Donn Vessels, Edward Wiley, John Wyatt, Kate Dougherty, Maggie Thrower, Whit Massengale, Isaiah Morgan, Pearlie Miller, , George Washington, Stella Carmichael, Mobilia Chestnut, Fred Clay, George McCampbell, Warren Henderson, Levia Harris, Florence Sherman, Dora Gaut, Ella Jordan, Helen Lyons, Nannie Carmichael, Ella Roddy, Ada Boysaw, Jennie O'Rear, Lillie Blakely, Cardo Baker and Tommie Durroh.

Professor W.J. Davenport, for whom a school would later be named. *Photograph courtesy of Jasper T. Duncan, "Activities Among Negroes," article in the* Chattanooga Times, *September 18, 1938.*

Room 2—Miss S.M. Fowler, Teacher:
Mellie Heggie, Docia Smith, Fred Durroh, Emma Powell, Clinton Whiteside, Nellie Heggie, Mary Blackburn, Emma Lynear, Maria Joseph, Willie Tyree, Ernest Smith, Annie Baker, Doreas Gooden, Katie Holland, Lillie Atkins, Andrew Massengill, Nora Moore, Spencer Clark, Stanford McKissick and Rosa Pitner.
Room 3—Miss F.N. Day, Teacher:
Mary Hawkins, Lena Crawford, Harriet Nelson, Indiana Jenkins, Percy Durroh, Charlie Miller, George Davis, Charlie Manning, Joseph Wade, Kelsey Edwards, Rufus Montgomery, Wesley Tyree, Wesley Franklin, Willie Walker, King Williams, Willie Arnold, Frank Scott, Salenia Drake, Lula Peet, Lavinia Burgess, Willia Grisham, Ida Davis, Gertrude Wiley, Sallie Edinburgh, Eddie Crawford, Lula Gilbreath, Sammie Young, Beulah Walker, Frank Dunn, Sadie May Jackson, Claude Burnet, Louisa Avery, Willie Pierce, Maggie Mitchell, John Hazelherd and Felix Hamilton.
Room 4—Miss S.L. Grant, Teacher:
Willie Scofield, Georgia Robertson, Mattie Boysaw, Ella Jamison, Sadie Moore, Mattie Scofield, Maggie Moore, Harry Massingale, John Johnson, Fredie Jones, George Mills, Benson Head, George Massingale, Colquett Lorthridge, George Millls and J.F. Calloway.

3.

Early African American Commerce

At the turn of the century when J. Bliss White was just penning his *1904 Biography and Achievements of the Colored Citizens of Chattanooga*, Chattanooga African Americans had just paid over $222,694 in taxes on personal properties—no small amount by any means. Collectively, the African American community owned church and societal properties valued at over $120,000.[35]

The city boasted as many as twenty or more privately owned African American grocery stores, including the Wester Brother's Grocery, owned by S.S. and W.H. Wester.[36] The Wester brothers even had a bakery attached to their grocery store, which the entire city patronized.

There were other businesses that African Americans could be proud of too, like Southern Stove and Holloware Manufacturing, which made its own stoves and holloware and shipped to states like Alabama, Mississippi and Georgia. The Rising Sun Manufacturing Company, located on Harrison Avenue and run by J.A. Strictland, also specialized in stoves, grate baskets, fenders and fronts, stove repair and holloware. The very business-minded Douglas McWharter was a major stockholder in the Rising Sun Manufacturing Company, and since he also owned extensive property throughout the city and a prosperous cotton farm on the side, the Rising Sun was sure to remain a business staple in the community.

African Americans in Chattanooga were so progressive that they even had their own "Colored" YMCA. Located at the corner of Georgia Avenue and East 9th Street, the "Colored" YMCA had been formed by the forward-thinking William M. Wilson. Wilson was another active, diverse thinker who had once been appointed deputy sheriff of the county, and who also served as a letter carrier for the post office.[37] His idea for a YMCA for African Americans was not well received at first, but later it was well supported by African Americans and whites alike.

Chattanooga African Americans also had their own progressive pharmacy. The East Side Pharmacy was located on the first floor of the modern James Building, which was owned by Dr. O.W. James. Dr. James and his partner, Mr. Allen, formed the James and Allen Drug Company, and together they supplied all the drugs in demand by the East Side Pharmacy. At one time, the East Side Pharmacy was considered the

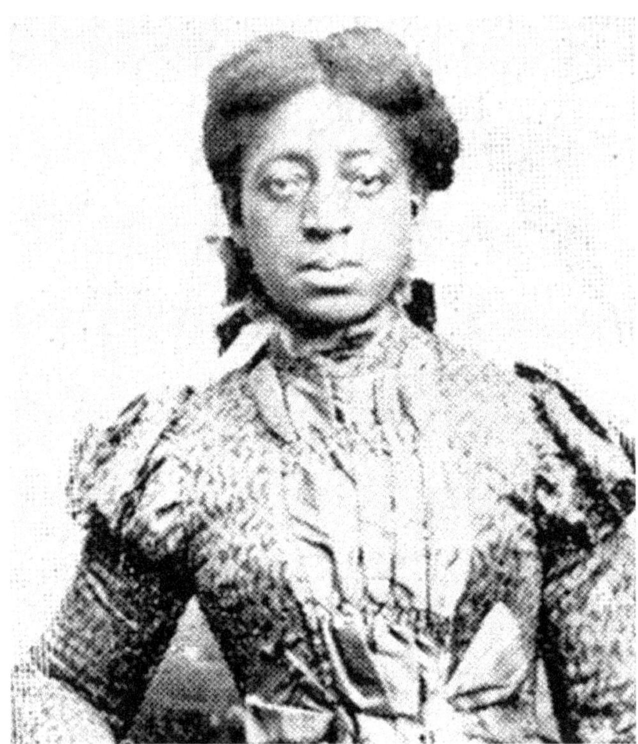

Mrs. N. Morton started a grocery and restaurant business on Boyce Street (Chestnut Street) with almost no money to her name. She built it into an extremely prosperous enterprise. *Photograph courtesy of* 1904 Biography and Achievements of the Colored Citizens of Chattanooga *by J. Bliss White.*

finest Negro drugstore in the entire United States, and Negro physicians and their patients frequented the establishment.

The prescriptions were filled by young pharmacist R. Emerson Andrews, a scholar graduate of Shaw University's Pharmaceutical Department. As the legend went, Andrews spoke Latin and Greek, excelled in mathematics and was so intellectually gifted, he graduated from Shaw's Pharmaceutical Department in 1893—at a very young age![38]

There were female entrepreneurs in Chattanooga too, such as Mrs. N. Morton. Morton came to Chattanooga "with practically nothing" and went on to build a very profitable grocery store and restaurant business at 217 Boyce Street. Morton was described as a "a striking example of what can be accomplished by our women of today without the aid or assistance of anyone."[39]

Part II

Notable People and Places

But as there are those either unwilling or unable to see other than spots in individual or national character, it is true wisdom that the Negro keep in the light, firmly assured that thorough investigation will cause wonder, not that there are spots, but that their number is so few in Negro character. Investigation, like many other excellent things, produces its best results only with the fullness of time.

...We feel that this work will not be found wanting in this its basic argument. We dedicate this book to the generation of mothers and fathers, now past or nearing the Great Divide, who toiled, and are toiling, without cessation and without thought of self, that their children might possess the golden keys that unlock the door of opportunity.

—*Excerpt from* 1904 Biography and Achievements of the Colored Citizens of Chattanooga, *by J. Bliss White.*

4.

Notable African Americans Who Had an Impact on the United States

William "Uncle Bill" Lewis and Andrew's Raiders

Uncle Bill Puts the Shackles on Andrew's Raiders

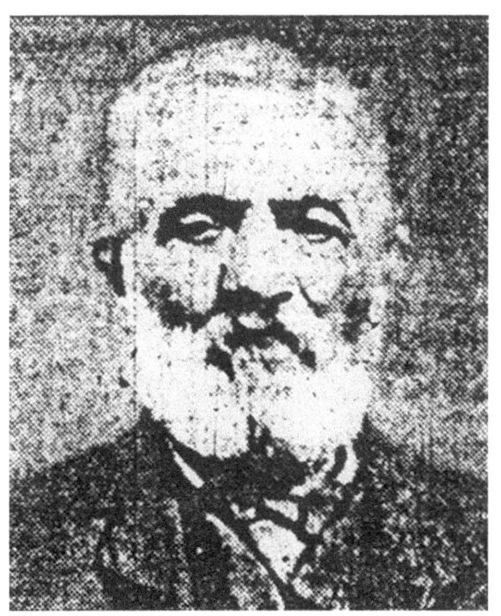

This is an early newspaper photograph of William "Uncle Bill" Lewis, Chattanooga's first African American blacksmith, and the man who put the shackles on Andrew's Raiders. *Photograph courtesy of the* Chattanooga Daily Times, *July 1, 1928, Jubilee No. 25.*

William "Uncle Bill" Lewis arrived at Ross's Landing in 1837 and set up shop on Georgia Avenue. He was the first African American blacksmith to locate to Chattanooga. He was a slave at the time of his arrival, but soon purchased his wife's freedom, his own freedom and the freedom of his family members.

When Uncle Bill was born into slavery in Winchester, Tennessee, in 1810, he belonged to a man by the name of Colonel Lewis. He was taught the blacksmithing trade as soon as he was old enough to learn and was so good at his job that he not only earned money for his owner, but he was also able to work at odd hours and save money for himself.

Not long after Uncle Bill married, he had saved enough money to buy his wife's freedom for $1,000. He did this because it was the law of the land that the children of slaves must follow the condition of their mothers, and Uncle Bill knew that if his wife was free, his descendants would also be free.

A *Chattanooga Times* newspaper article dated September 18, 1938, described Uncle Bill as honest, industrious and faithful, so much so that his owners allowed him to move to Chattanooga in 1837 and set up a blacksmith shop on Georgia Avenue. Uncle Bill purchased this time to operate on his own for $350 a year.

According to the eighth census (1860) population schedules and worksheets, there were ninety-nine other free Negroes in Chattanooga, Tennessee, at the time that Uncle Bill made Chattanooga his home. These other free Negroes were employed as day laborers, farmhands, washerwomen, seamstresses and draymen, but Uncle Bill was the most important of the group in terms of skills.

In fact, Uncle Bill's name is mentioned in early documentation about the little town of Chattanooga, Tennessee. He is said to have been the man who forged the bell that rang out in the lone log building in the middle of the growing community. The building stood on a lot somewhere between 4th and 5th Streets, near Georgia Avenue and was used for community gatherings, school sessions and other services. Approximately sixteen by twenty feet in size, the little building was made of logs, chinked and daubed with mud. It had a stick and mud chimney, and in the middle of the chimney was the pestle and mortar that had been forged with Uncle Bill's own hands. By striking the mortar with the pestle, the community was alerted to public meetings.

Aside from his community services, Uncle Bill made a steady amount of money shodding horses and grounding iron. He had already begun making payments on his own freedom, and not long after his arrival in Chattanooga, he made the final payment on his papers. He paid a total of $1,000 for the right to live as a free man.

There are conflicting reports about what he did next. It has been reported that he proceeded to buy his six-year-old son for $400. Since he had already purchased his wife's freedom, and her freedom secured the status of any children she had thereafter, it is assumed that this son was born before Uncle Bill finished paying for his wife. Nevertheless, by 1851 he had also purchased his mother and his aunt for $150 each, a small sum because they were both elderly. He then purchased his two brothers for $1,000 each, and enlisted the help of a slave trader to buy his sister for the bargain price of $400.

In total, Uncle Bill spent $5,100 to free himself and his family, an amount equal to well over $100,000 in the new millennium.

Since the laws of his day forbade Uncle Bill to do business in his own name, he had to pay a white man to legalize all his transactions. But the man was happy to do this service for him. Chattanoogans knew Uncle Bill as "a rugged man of much intelligence, and one who always bore an excellent name for thrift, honesty and sobriety."[40]

Uncle Bill became famous when, during the Civil War and the battles for Chattanooga, he put the shackles on Andrew's Raiders. Andrew's Raiders were a group of Union soldiers led by Union Capt. James J. Andrews, who stole the famous locomotive, "The General." They planned to use the train to burn bridges between Atlanta and Chattanooga to prepare for an attack on Tennessee by the Union Army.

The Andrew's Raiders were captured and confined to Swaim's Jail, an old African American slave jail once located on what is now a Provident Insurance Company parking lot. (See page 118 for a photograph and description of Swaim's Jail.) According to various eyewitness testimonies, it was Uncle Bill's son who was called into the dungeon of the jail to rivet a pair of heavy iron fetters around the ankles of the expedition leader, and Uncle Bill supervised his efforts.

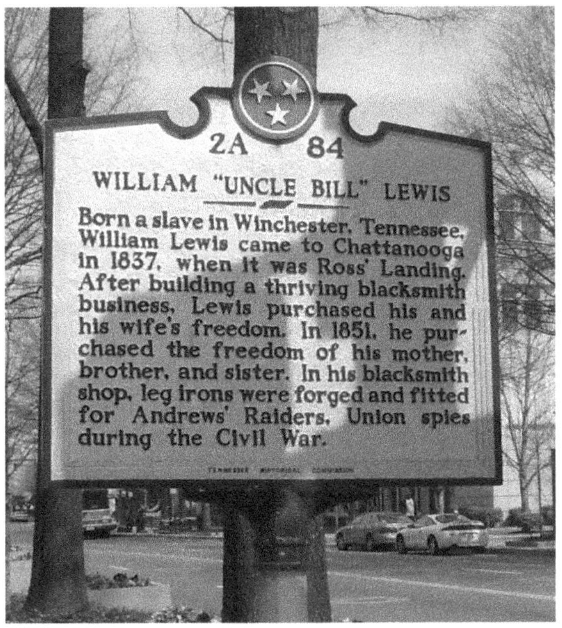

A snapshot of the historical marker located on Market Street in downtown Chattanooga that was erected to honor Uncle Bill's memory. It is a fond reminder of Uncle Bill's contributions to Chattanooga and its development. *Photograph courtesy of Rita Lorraine Hubbard, ©March 2007.*

Uncle Bill lived in a large two-story frame house about a block from Swaim's Jail, and though he was the man responsible for putting the shackles on the raiders, he also befriended them. He raised a large quantity of lettuce in his yard and obtained permission to send some of it to the prisoners.

Uncle Bill was extremely prosperous. His blacksmithing business did well and he was able to pay for his house and accumulate a large amount of money. In 1850 at age thirty-nine, he had reported his real estate worth to a census taker at $1,500 (roughly equivalent to $35,116 in the new millennium). However, by 1860 he reported a worth of $7,000 (equivalent to over $150,000).

Uncle Bill hired workers to help operate his shop, and his excellent skills as a blacksmith even earned him enough money to send several of his nine children north to be educated. In fact, his son, H.B. Lewis, was educated at Howard University in Washington, D.C., and eventually became a letter carrier. Uncle Bill also sent three daughters up North to be educated. They remained in the North, married and started families there.

Uncle Bill also had a daughter named Sudie Winkler who taught in the Chattanooga city school system; a son named George who was also a blacksmith and was the son who put the shackles on the Andrew's Raiders under Uncle Bill's supervision; another daughter who was a milliner and a grandson born and raised in Chattanooga who eventually moved to Paris, France, and conducted a successful orchestra there.

Uncle Bill remained in business for many years, blacksmithing and wagon-making for the citizens of Chattanooga, Tennessee, and leaving a lasting impression upon everyone he met.

Uncle Bill died on September 2, 1896. He lived a full life and was much loved by both African Americans and whites in the city of Chattanooga. He did the community proud not only through his industry and entrepreneurial spirit, but also through the kindness he showed to persons like Andrew's Raiders, even though he met them in their darkest hour.

Private Hubbard D. Pryor of the 44th U.S. Colored Infantry

His Recruiting Poster Gained National Interest

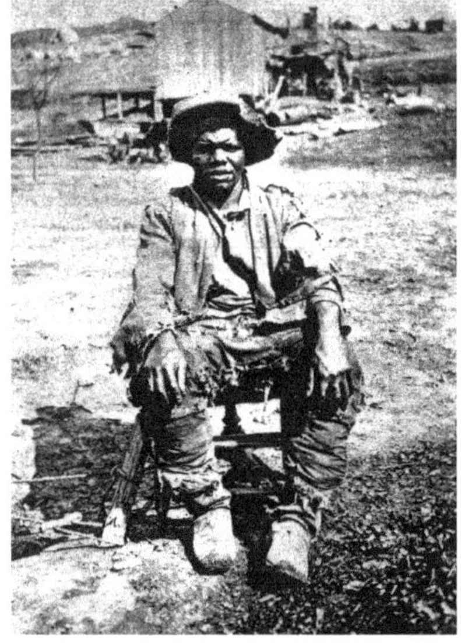

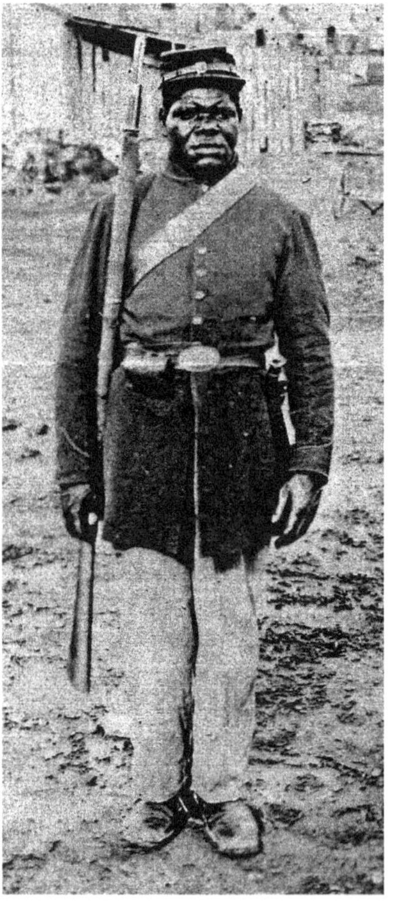

Hubbard Pryor was a twenty-two-year-old ex-slave who fled Polk County, Georgia, and his owner, Haden Pryor. His goal was to cross the border into Tennessee and join the Federal soldiers who were currently stationed in Chattanooga.

Hubbard arrived in Chattanooga on April 7, 1864, hungry, exhausted and determined to be free. His legs were swaddled with thick strips of old cloth…necessary after the vicious and bloody attack by the bloodhounds his master had used to track him. But Hubbard made it into Chattanooga anyway and after rest, food and medical care, he quickly enlisted in the 44th U.S. Colored Infantry, a company organized by Colonel Thomas J. Morgan. There he not only learned to be a soldier, he also received instruction in reading, writing and self-respect. Hubbard and the 44th saw action at Walden's Ridge, and later marched through Ringgold and Dalton, Georgia, all the way to Rome, Georgia. He and his company constructed a fort in Dalton and quickly prepared to skirmish with Confederate General Joseph Wheeler and his regiments, who suddenly appeared and demanded that the 44th surrender to them. When the 44th refused to surrender, the Confederate general withdrew his ultimatum and there was no battle.

By October 13, 1864, Hubbard and the 44th had returned to Dalton, Georgia, to continue their military duties. Unfortunately, they were surrounded by Confederate General John B. Hood's entire army. The two regiments skirmished, but the 44th was definitely outnumbered and General Hood

At one time in history these before-and-after photographs of Private Hubbard Pryor were a popular—and quite effective—marketing tool for military recruitment.

Top: Hubbard Pryor as he arrived in Chattanooga, Tennessee, on April 7, 1864.

Bottom: PFC Hubbard Pryor a few days later, after joining the 44th U.S. Colored Infantry.

Both photographs courtesy of the National Archives.

demanded that they surrender, promising "no quarter"—or rather no mercy if they did not.

The 44th preferred to fight; they were not the only Negro regiment who had heard about the atrocities of the Fort Pillow Massacre in which unarmed Negroes had been slaughtered after they surrendered to General Nathan B. Forrest. However, because they were outnumbered, their commanding officers felt that surrender was the best course.

Upon their surrender, Hubbard and the other Negro soldiers were immediately separated from the white officers in their regiment. The Confederates regarded all Negro prisoners as recaptured slaves, and the Negro men of the 44th were no different. They were immediately stripped of their shoes and uniforms and put to work for the Confederates.

Of course, recapture could not crush Hubbard's spirit. He had escaped once, and given time he would escape again! Luckily, he did not have to. Emancipation was not far behind the capture of the 44th U.S. Colored Infantry, and once the slaves were set free, Private Hubbard Pryor got married, became a farmer and had three sons and a daughter.

Hubbard's Civil War pension records document his eventual move from Georgia to Calvert, Texas. There he lived to be forty-eight years old. It is not immediately known how he died.

Hinton D. Alexander

One of the Original Jubilee Singers of International Fame

Hinton D. Alexander was a native of Chattanooga, Tennessee. He was a young man when he was sent to Fisk University in Nashville in the early 1870s.

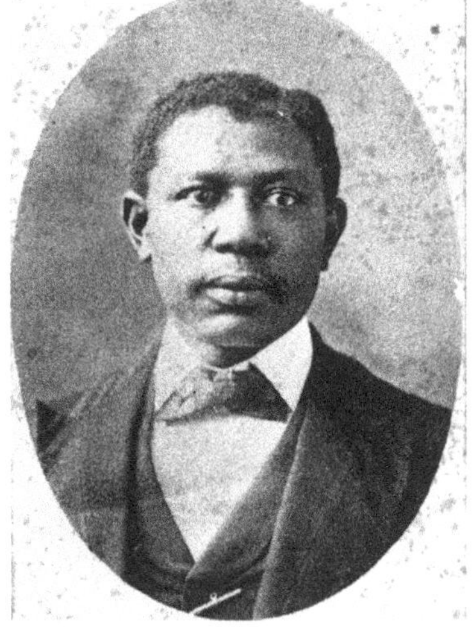

This is an 1882 photograph of Hinton D. Alexander, an original Fisk Jubilee Singer and the first Negro in Chattanooga to go to college. *Photograph courtesy of the Paul A. Heiner Collection, 1882.*

Of historical note is the fact that Alexander was the first African American on record in Chattanooga, Tennessee to go to college. At that time, Fisk was a new school that was established in a war barracks by the American Missionary Association. A Northerner by the name of George T. White was serving as Fisk Jubilee treasurer and was directing music at the time that Alexander entered school. It did not take him long to discover Alexander's beautiful voice and make him a member of the Fisk Jubilee Singers, a group that toured America and Europe singing Negro spirituals and jubilee melodies.

The Jubilee Singers left Fisk University on October 6, 1871, under White's Leadership and spent seven years of "continuous labor" in the United States, Great Britain, Ireland, Holland, Germany and Switzerland. Jubilee Hall—the beautiful building they were working

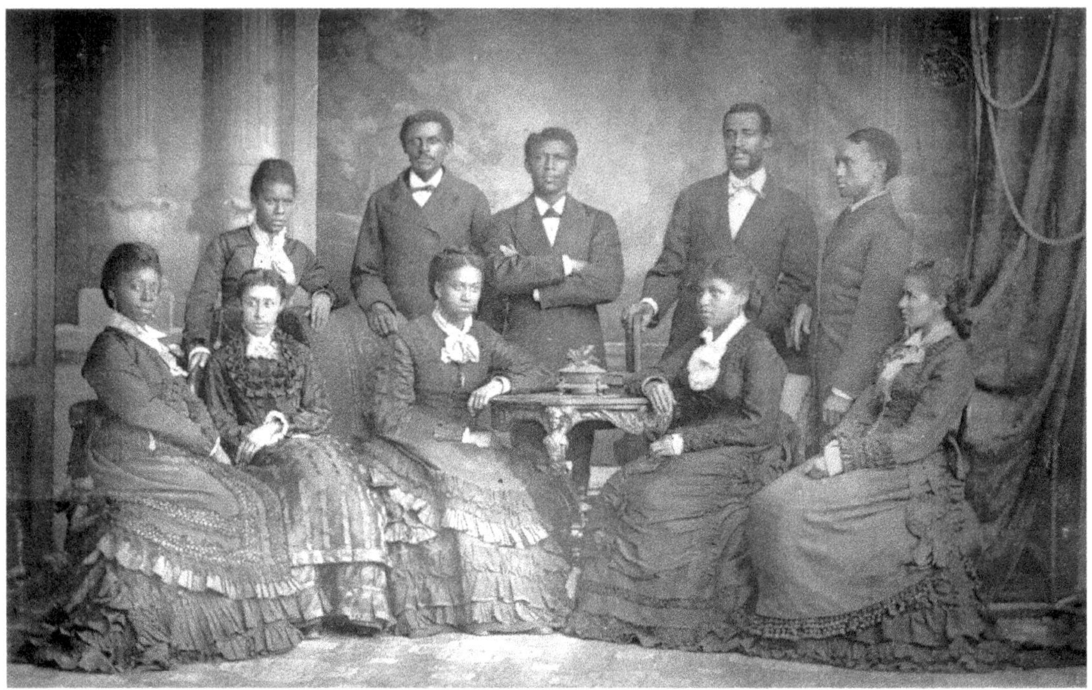

Here is yet another photograph of Hinton D. Alexander, this time posing with the original Fisk Jubilee Singers. Alexander is standing in the middle of the photograph with his arms folded. *Photograph courtesy of the John Hope and Aurelia Elizabeth Franklin Library Special Collections, ©1875.*

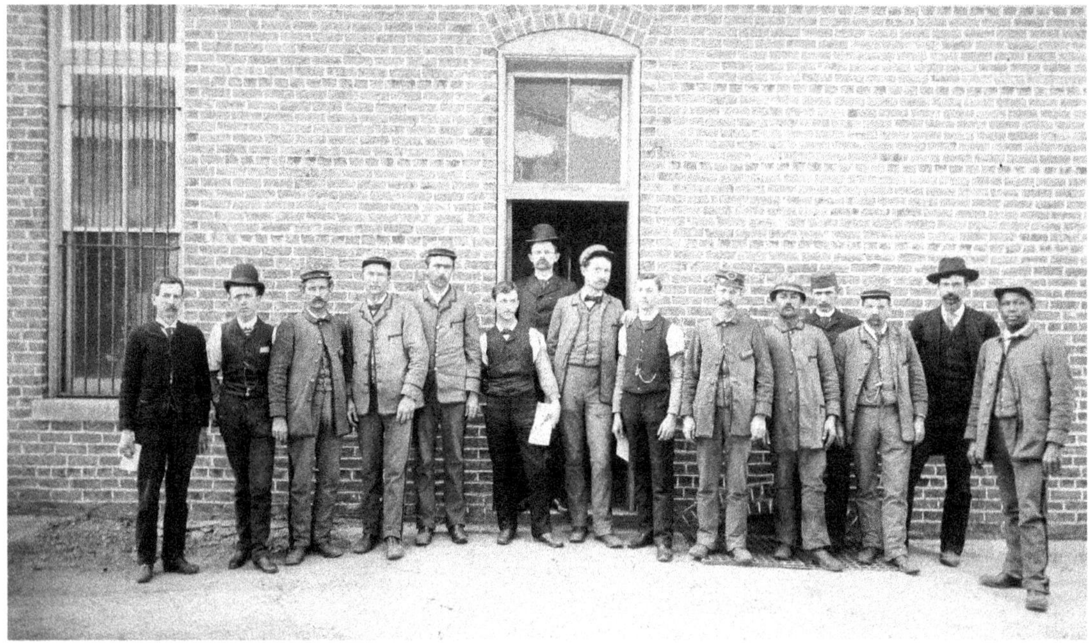

This photograph of Hinton D. Alexander and other postal carriers was taken in front of the Carter Street Post Office. Alexander, standing at the far right, was the only African American in the photograph. He served the *Chattanooga Times* building for many years. *Photograph courtesy of the Paul A. Heiner Collection, 1887.*

so hard to raise money for—would become the home for young women and female teachers at Fisk University.

After Hinton D. Alexander completed his tenure as a Fisk Jubilee Singer, he returned to Chattanooga and became a mail carrier for the Carter Street Post Office. Alexander served as a carrier from 1883 until 1921.

Hinton D. Alexander died on October 13, 1926, and was buried in Forest Hills Cemetery, #16862, Section 5, Lot 200. The inscription on his tombstone reads: "This Memorial erected by the Chattanooga Band of Hope, in memory of Supt. H.D. Alexander, in Appreciation of 40 Yrs. Faithful Service. His works do follow him."

Roland Hayes

The First African American Man Ever to Win International Fame as a Concert Performer

Roland Hayes was born on a farm near Calhoun, Georgia, on June 3, 1887. His parents, Fanny and William Hayes, were former slaves. When Roland was only eleven years old, his father died suddenly. His mother decided to move to Chattanooga—a city that was considered to be progressive—and there she would try to make a better life.

In Chattanooga, Hayes attended school and worked in the Chattanooga foundries to help his mother take care of the family. But he also sang on the streets for pennies, captivating his audiences with the haunting African American spirituals handed down to him from generations past. His voice was so impressive that a music teacher offered to give him music lessons. Unfortunately, the extra money Hayes made singing on the streets simply was not enough to help his family and he had to drop out of school and find other jobs to supplement the family income. He left school without even finishing the sixth grade.

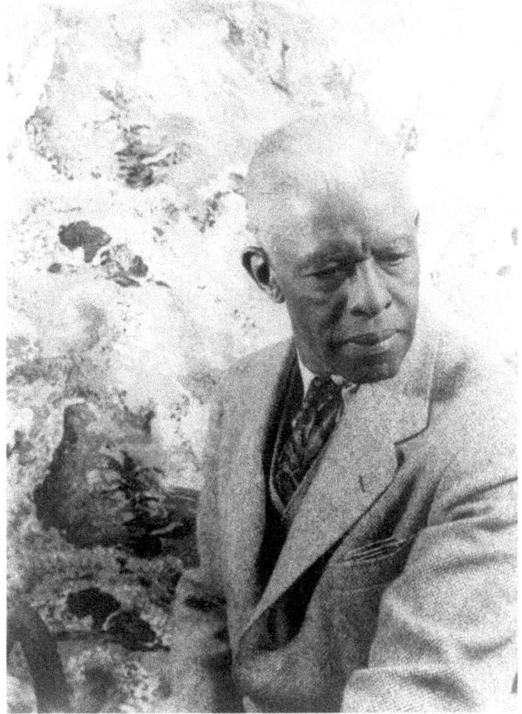

A 1954 photograph of Roland Hayes, the first African American man ever to win international fame as a concert performer. *Photograph courtesy of the Library of Congress, Prints & Photographs Division, Carl Van Vechten Collection.*

At age twenty, Hayes enrolled in Fisk University in Nashville, Tennessee, where he became a member of the Fisk Jubilee Singers. Later, he moved to Louisville, Kentucky, and worked as a singer in a silent movie theatre, singing his tunes offstage so that moviegoers could hear his voice but did not have to look upon the color of his skin. While he was there, the president of Fisk University made contact with him and asked him to be lead tenor for the Fisk Jubilee Singers on their Boston tour.

After the tour, Hayes decided not return to Fisk; rather, he stayed in Boston and planned his entertainment career. He saved his money, rented the Symphony Hall in Boston and gave dazzling concert performances. He was a pioneer in the entertainment industry in that he was his own concert manager—something almost unheard of in those days. Hayes took sole responsibility in arranging and promoting his own concerts.

In time, Hayes was so popular that he was invited to perform at many great houses in America, including Carnegie Hall. By 1920, he performed his very first European concert in London England. While he was there, King George and Queen Mary of England requested that he come and sing for them. This son of ex-slaves with the meager education was standing before kings and queens!

Hayes toured Europe many times, singing his beautiful songs in seven different languages. By the late 1920s, he was the highest-paid tenor in the world. But Hayes had other talents too. Many of the spirituals he performed had never before been set to music, and Roland Hayes arranged them for orchestral accompaniment himself.

Hayes was a very successful man. He and wife Helen and daughter Afrika maintained homes in both Massachusetts and Georgia. His Georgia residence was the very same beautiful six-hundred-acre farm where Hayes's own mother had once lived as a slave and where she had given birth to him.

After a racial incident left Hayes badly beaten and landed both him and his wife in jail, the Hayes family moved out of Georgia and sold their beautiful farm. Hayes spent his latter years mentoring young musicians, teaching at Boston University and receiving numerous doctoral degrees and awards, including the NAACP-Spingarn Medal.

In 1991, Roland Hayes, the son of ex-slaves with the sixth-grade education, was posthumously inducted into the Georgia Music Hall of Fame. In 1995, the Georgia Department of Natural Resources erected an historical marker in Hayes's honor. The marker site is now designated as the Roland Hayes Park, and State Highway 156 West in Calhoun, Georgia, is named Roland Hayes Parkway.

Ed Johnson

His Lynching Launched Federalism

Unfortunately, not every Chattanooga African American whose life impacted the United States was able to make that impact in a positive way. This sad fact especially applied to the life of Ed Johnson.

On Monday, March 19, 1906, Ed Johnson, a young African American male living in Chattanooga, Tennessee, was hanged on the Walnut Street Bridge by a white mob bent on "justice." Johnson had been accused, arrested, tried and convicted of raping a young white woman by the name of Nevada Taylor, and although she had never had the opportunity to see her rapist and therefore could not positively identify him, he was hanged anyway.

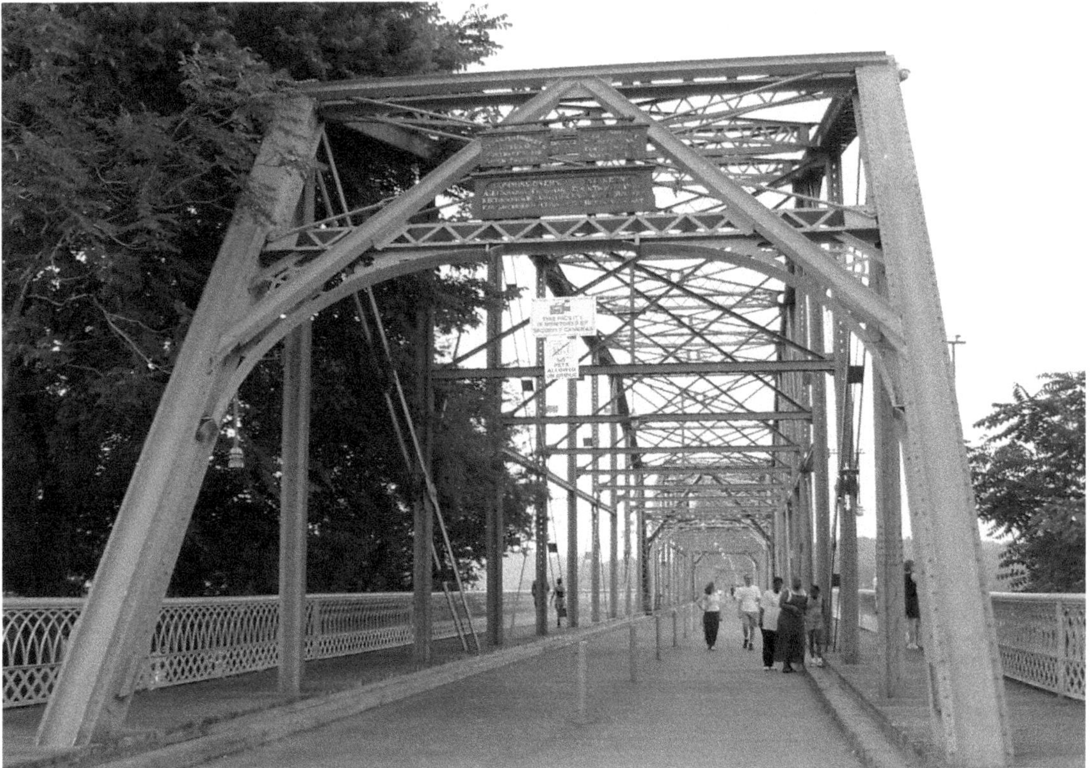

This is a photograph of the Walnut Street Bridge where young Ed Johnson was lynched in 1906. It is now used as a walking bridge in Chattanooga, Tennessee. *Photograph courtesy of Rita Lorraine Hubbard, ©2004.*

Born in 1882, Johnson was not originally from Chattanooga, Tennessee. Very little is known about him, his family or where they came from. He lived with his father, who was called "Skinbone" because of his skinny frame. Johnson also had a sister, but it is unknown whether she also lived with their father.

Johnson did not have much of an education and reportedly never even finished the fourth grade. He had no special skills, preferring to work with his hands. He enjoyed carpentry and performing such work as roofing and janitorial duties. It is also known that he helped someone do roofing work for two churches, and that he also assisted in working on additions to three houses. In addition, Johnson was known to work in the Last Chance Saloon from time to time, performing such duties as mopping and tending to the pool tables. Most of the time, he exchanged his manual labor for food and a place to sleep.

Johnson's simple life changed the night young Nevada Taylor started out for home after a long day's work. Taylor lived near the Forest Hills Cemetery at the foot of Lookout Mountain. Even though her home was well within sight and shouting distance when the attack occurred, no one in the neighborhood saw or heard anything. Someone simply slipped up behind her and tightened a leather strap around her neck. She quickly lost consciousness, and when she awoke her clothing was disheveled. Only later, as a doctor examined her in the safety of her own home, did she discover that she had been raped.

Taylor had not seen her attacker so she had no idea whether he was white or black. At first nothing came of the case, but when a reward of $375 was offered, a white witness quickly came forward and said he saw Johnson in that particular area around the time of the rape.

Unfortunately for Johnson, the moment he was identified as being "in the area," his fate was sealed. He insisted on his innocence, but no one was interested in hearing his side of the story. He was quickly appointed two trial lawyers, but they had never even handled a criminal case before. The lawyers tried to do right by Johnson; they immediately requested enough time to adequately investigate and research the case, but their request was promptly denied.

A mob had attempted to lynch Johnson during this time, but Judge McReynolds—who presided over the proceedings—had sent him to Nashville to be certain he lived to go to trial. The night of this first lynching attempt two members of the unruly mob were accidentally shot and one was stabbed in the frenzy to get to Johnson. In an attempt to calm the crowd and keep them from further hurting themselves, Judge McReynolds allowed five men to accompany him through the jail to prove that Johnson was no longer there. Once the men were satisfied, they dispersed. As unruly as they had been, not a single member of the mob was arrested.

As the trial drew near, an all-white jury was chosen—which was definitely no coincidence. The evidence indicated that the judge and the court officials had taken measures to be certain that no black man would be called to serve in the case. This, of course, was a violation of the Fourteenth Amendment, which stated that any states or counties that systematically kept black people out of the jury pool were violating the equal protections clause.

Nevertheless, Johnson was quickly tried by the all-white jury, and was convicted and sentenced to death for the crime of rape. Soon after his conviction, Skinbone, his father, approached attorneys Noah Walter Parden and Styles Linton Hutchins and asked them to appeal Ed's conviction. They did, traveling to the Supreme Court to argue for a stay of execution until the facts of the case could be investigated.

This act—arguing for a stay of execution before the Supreme Court—set several precedents. First of all, this was the first time an African American—Noah Parden, in this case—had ever argued for a stay of execution in the Supreme Court. This was also the first time that a stay of execution was granted for an African American. Additionally, it marked the first time that an African American was designated as lead counsel in a Supreme Court case. As fate would have it, however, Noah Parden would never get to argue the case before the Supreme Court justices, because Johnson was lynched anyway.

On that fateful night, the lynch mob began marching from the St. Elmo area all the way to the courthouse. Word spread quickly that the mob was approaching, but nothing was done. These men were furious that the Supreme Court had agreed to a stay of execution. In their minds, outsiders were trying to influence the way they meted out justice to the Negroes in their own city, and this was unacceptable.

The men burst through the jail doors and reportedly sent Sheriff Shipp to the restroom. Then they dragged Johnson out, beat him, marched him to the Walnut

Street Bridge and hanged him. The lynching was a brutal one, because Johnson did not die right away. The men eventually opened fire on him.

Sheriff Joseph F. Shipp was accused of conspiring with a mob to kill Ed Johnson. According to various accounts, Sheriff Shipp knew a mob was forming to lynch Ed hours before he was killed, but refused to send guard reinforcements to the jail and failed to do anything to disperse the crowd. When the mob arrived at the jail, they simply "suggested" that Shipp go to the bathroom and remain there, and he took their advice without protest. Johnson was left unprotected and fell victim to the mob.

Sheriff Shipp was later tried for his role in the lynching by the Federal government. He served ninety days in prison for conspiracy involving a murder. His trial and conviction would make him a local hero in Chattanooga, whose white citizens insisted he had done nothing wrong. He returned to Chattanooga to a shower of praise on January 30, 1910.

Styles L. Hutchins

First African American Admitted to the Georgia Bar; First Chattanooga African American Admitted to a State Office

Styles Linton Hutchins was born on November 21, 1852, in Lawrenceville, Georgia. His father's great talent as an artist brought much money into the home, and Hutchins was able to enjoy a good college education because of it. He completed his studies at Atlanta University and devoted his time to teaching until 1871.

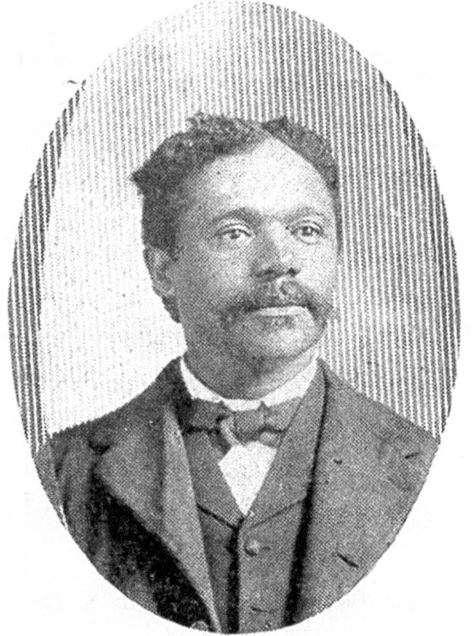

This is a 1904 photograph of Attorney Styles Linton Hutchins, who was the first Chattanooga African American admitted to a state office and the first African American admitted to the Georgia Bar. *Photograph courtesy of* 1904 Biography and Achievements of the Colored Citizens of Chattanooga *by J. Bliss White.*

At that time, Hutchins exchanged his teaching abilities for a position as principal of the Knox Institute in Athens, Georgia. Under his expert supervision, the institute flourished, increasing to the size of six hundred students and seven teachers.

In 1873 Hutchins resigned from his position as principal and moved to South Carolina, where he earned enough money to enter the University of Columbia, South Carolina's law department. He graduated in 1876 and was admitted to practice before the Supreme Court of South Carolina. He later served as a judge in that same state, but soon resigned because of the politics of the day. He then moved to Atlanta, Georgia, and demanded to be allowed to practice law there.

Georgia legislature had previously passed an act requiring that lawyers from other states undergo an examination at the discretion of the presiding judge before they could practice. This way, the legislature could keep unwanted lawyers—such as men of color—from practicing. Hutchins fought this racial opposition for six months, and was finally admitted to the bar. He went down on record as the first African American ever to be admitted to the Georgia Bar.

By 1881, Hutchins had grown tired of Georgia customs and moved to Chattanooga where he immediately began to practice law. Although white lawyers often referred to him as flamboyant and rebellious, he did hold the esteem and admiration of both judges and members of the bar.

In 1882, Hutchins joined other African Americans in Chattanooga in organizing and establishing the *Independent Age* newspaper. He served as editor of this newspaper, which was the only newspaper whose press and outfit were owned and operated entirely by African American men in Chattanooga.

By 1886, Hutchins was elected to the Tennessee legislature, triumphing over one of the most popular white Democrats of that time. This election made him the first Chattanooga African American admitted to a State Office. He held this seat until 1888, and then resumed practicing law.

In 1901, Hutchins was ordained a minister, though he never assumed any ministerial duties. At the time this photograph was taken, he had practiced law for thirty years and was considered the pioneer Negro lawyer of the South.

Hutchins would go on to help Noah Parden represent Ed Johnson, a young African American male accused of raping a white woman.

Styles Linton Hutchins, born November 21, 1852, died on September 7, 1950—a teacher, notary public and Negro pioneer lawyer.

RANDOLPH MILLER

Ex-Slave and Editor of The Blade, *a Nationally Syndicated Newspaper*

According to *Standard History of Chattanooga* by Charles D. McGuffey, Randolph Miller was born a slave in Fluvanna County, Virginia, in 1842, and belonged to Dr. Robert W. Curran. When he was nine years old, he was taken to Georgia with "a drove of Negroes" and sold to Andrew Jackson Miller.

When General William T. Sherman's army marched through Georgia, they took young Randolph Miller with them. Miller came to Chattanooga in 1864 as a ward of the army, and stayed on after the Civil War. He worked several odd jobs, finally landing a job with the *Chattanooga Daily Gazette*. His job was to "turn the press by muscular power." He later went to the American Union to try out his skill as a pressman operating a Washington press.

Miller returned to Chattanooga after the *Daily Times* was established. He worked for the *Daily Times* and the *Commercial*, finally landing a job with the *Times* as a pressman. He was taught to use a power press by George M. Day—a white man—and after he learned the inner workings of a newspaper, he soon launched his own paper.

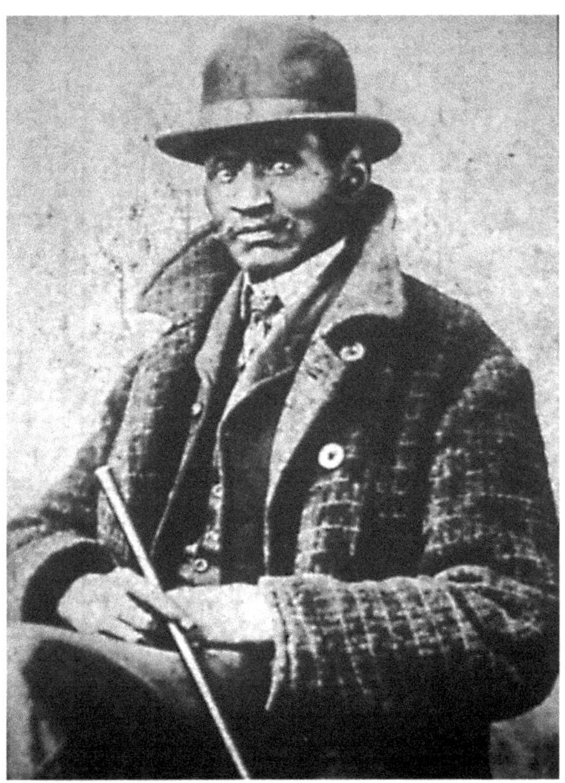

Randolph M. Miller, looking focused and prosperous. *Photograph courtesy of the* Chattanooga Daily Times, *July 1, 1928, Jubilee No. 32.*

He called his paper *The Blade.* Although Miller was considered "eccentric and illiterate," he soon became one of the most quoted editors in the entire country. Thousands of his quotes, which were known as "Gems from *The Blade*" and "Flashes from *The Blade*" were reprinted.

Miller was a fiery, outspoken man. He was like an early prototype for the civil rights leaders of the 1960s and 1970s, and he was certainly not afraid to speak out against the prejudice, injustice and segregation theories of the early days. In July 1905 he joined forces with other Chattanooga African American businessmen to launch a streetcar boycott against the Jim Crow laws regarding transportation, not knowing that this boycott would be considered an important move for early Tennessee civil rights, and would be celebrated in the history books over one hundred years later.

In 1905, segregation laws—or Jim Crow Laws as they were called—had already begun spreading across the state. Laws were already in place regarding the railway system, and when they spread to the streetcar systems of Tennessee in 1905, African Americans throughout the state began to speak of organizing boycotts in protest. In fact, there was not a major city in the state of Tennessee that did not experience some type of public display from the African American communities and their reaction to the extension of Jim Crow. Chattanooga was no exception.

Miller and other Chattanooga African American businessmen planned to start their own bus company so that African Americans could be transported with dignity and respect. They began by originating a system of hack lines that traveled between the city and the outlying black communities of Churchville, St. Elmo, Fort Cheatham and Tannery Flats. The first day of operation fell on July 16, with what some in the city described as "three vehicles of sorry appearance"[41] that carted members of the African American community about the city.

It is unknown whether the vehicles were as sorry as they were described, but it is known that Miller and the other hack operators found a loyal patronage among Chattanooga African Americans. The hack line vehicles ran almost to capacity, and Miller and his partners were so encouraged by this patronage that they applied for a

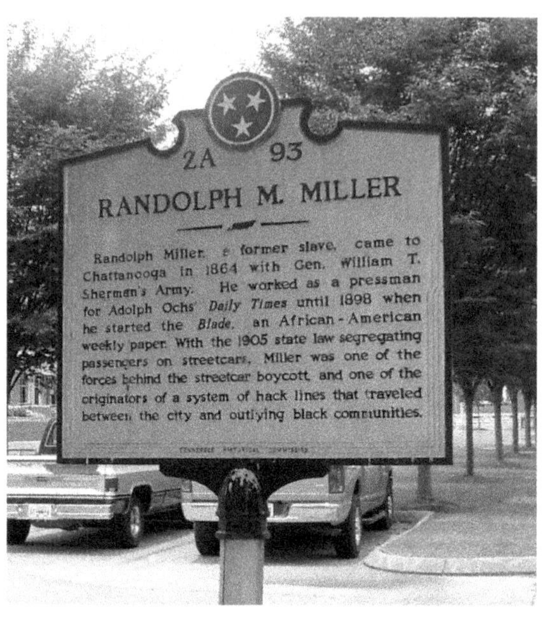

Today Randolph M. Miller's historical marker is proudly displayed in front of the beautiful Bessie Smith Museum on M.L. King Boulevard. *Photograph courtesy of Rita Lorraine Hubbard, ©2004.*

charter on August 29. Their charter named their new transportation company the Transfer Omnibus Motor Car Company. With an initial investment of $10,000, they devised a workable plan to replace the hack lines with several forty-passenger motor cars."[42]

Of course, they would need much more than the initial $10,000 investment to obtain the motor cars. They had thought to follow a similar plan as the one that had found success in Nashville, Tennessee; they would rely on small investments from a large number of black stockholders,[43] and would obtain the money they needed to make the purchases. Unfortunately, many of Chattanooga's African American leaders of that day were slow to give their public support to this bold venture, and this greatly hindered the success of the new transportation company.

Still, all was not lost. The four hack lines had a steady flow of customers. These customers had found their treatment on the public streetcars unbearable and preferred to pay the five-cent fare on the hack lines. This source of income could have eventually helped the businessmen reach their goal, but white officials felt that Miller and his partners were promoting "the spirit of resentment," and they made no secret about the fact that they wanted to close off these funds. Then, county humane officer W.J. Eddings announced that he intended to prosecute the hack operators for "working old worn-out animals from early morning until late at night and…only half feeding them,"[44] and it became glaringly apparent that the company would not be able to stand under such opposition.

The dream of an independent transportation system had been effectively crushed, but Randolph Miller was not afraid to speak out. In an October 1905 issue of *The Blade,* he said:

> *They have taken our part of the library; they have moved our school to the frog pond; they have passed the Jim Crow law; they have knocked us out of the jury box; they have played the devil generally, and what in thunder more will they do no one knows.*[45]

And so, the Transfer Omnibus Motor Car Company died away before its founders could determine whether it would be able to meet its high aspirations. The fiery Randolph Miller died in 1915, but the *Chattanooga Times* continued to reprint excerpts from his editorials. Today, Randolph M. Miller's historical marker is proudly displayed in front of the beautiful Bessie Smith Museum/African American History Museum, located on M.L. King Boulevard.

Noah Parden

First African American Lawyer to Argue and Win a Stay of Execution from the Supreme Court

Noah Walter Parden was born in Floyd County, Georgia, in 1865. By age seven, both his parents were dead and he was found abandoned on the doorstep of a Georgia orphanage.

Parden came to Chattanooga in 1884 and entered Howard High School in 1885. As a teenager and young adult, he worked days in a tobacco field and nights in a factory to save money for law school. He graduated from Howard High School after five years of hard work, and in late 1890, he entered Central Tennessee College of Nashville's law department.

Parden graduated law school at the head of his class and then returned to Chattanooga to set up practice. He was admitted to practice law in all courts in Tennessee, and the state supreme court in 1894. He was admitted to practice in the United States Supreme Court in 1895.

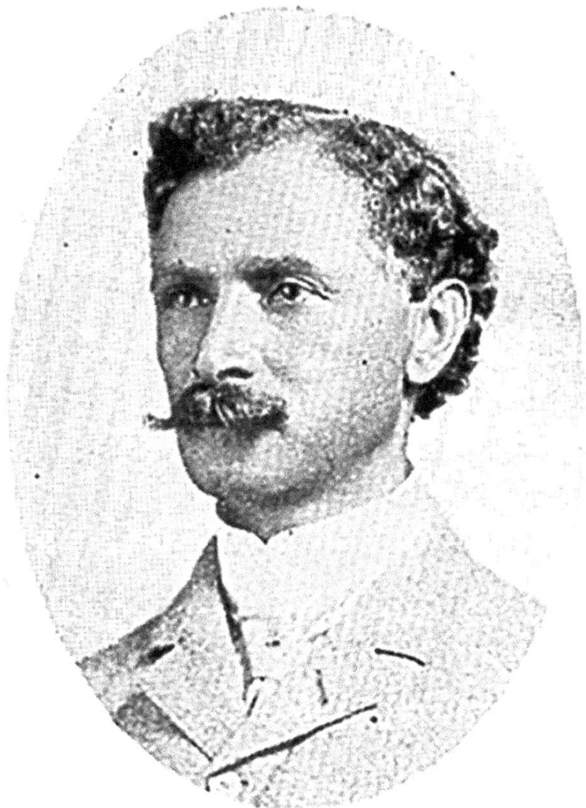

This is a 1904 photograph of Attorney Noah W. Parden, who was the first African American lawyer designated to serve as lead counsel before the Supreme Court. *Photograph courtesy of* 1904 Biography and Achievements of the Colored Citizens of Chattanooga *by J. Bliss White.*

Chattanooga's legal and civilian community referred to Noah Parden as a "trouble maker and community agitator," because he fought vigorously for his clients.[46] He was a notoriously passionate man and cried with the families when his clients were sentenced to prison, and he even cited complete chapters from Psalms and Proverbs or used parables from the New Testament to argue his point to the juries.

Parden believed strongly in God, and often kneeled in the back of the courtroom and prayed with his clients. He took on giants like insurance companies that sold policies to African Americans then routinely denied their claims because they believed African Americans were too poor to sue them. Parden usually won his cases, appealing to the white jurors to ask themselves the vital question that if the companies were allowed to defraud African Americans, who could be next on the list except white people?

For all of this devotion to his clients, Parden often received only a home cooked meal for payment. This was because most African Americans of that day were too poor to pay for representation, and those whites who were wealthy enough to pay would never go to an African American for representation in the first place. So Parden's practice was limited to those of his own race, most of whom just didn't earn enough money (if they worked at all) to pay him what he deserved.

Parden rectified this dilemma by becoming one of the earliest lawyers on record to use the "contingency" method of collecting fees for representation. He would take on a case against such culprits as the large insurance companies mentioned earlier, free of charge. If he won the case (which he usually did) he was entitled to a predetermined percentage of the award, which he collected before the client ever received the money. If he lost the case, the client could then go ahead and serve him the hot home cooked meal at their family's dinner table as payment.

Parden would go on to represent Ed Johnson, a young African American male accused of raping a white woman in 1906. When Johnson was convicted of the crime and sentenced to die, Parden became part of a team of lawyers who filed an appeal with the United States Supreme Court for a stay of execution until the facts could be investigated. Parden himself argued for the stay of execution. This act in itself was an historic event, because before that time no other African American had ever been allowed to argue anything before the Supreme Court justices.

Parden's argument was most effective, and Justice Harlan agreed to the stay. He even designated Parden "lead counsel," another historic event, since no African American had ever been considered a lead counsel before that time. Unfortunately, when the citizens of Chattanooga heard about the stay, a mob formed and took matters into their own hands. They hanged Johnson on the Walnut Street Bridge before Parden could argue the case.

Neither Noah Walter Parden nor Styles Linton Hutchins ever returned to Chattanooga, Tennessee after the lynching. Parden had been in Washington, D.C., arguing the case, and Hutchins had been out of the city when the lynching occurred. Both attorneys received word of the lynching, and were told of the violent rumors circulating that they themselves would be lynched the moment they showed their faces in the city. Both Parden and Hutchins moved their families to Oklahoma.

Despite the outcome of the Ed Johnson case, Noah Parden's law career was an outstanding one. It is documented that he won scores of lawsuits. A white lawyer from Chattanooga once told a local newspaper:

> *Even though he* [Noah Parden] *is black and they're white, Noah Parden develops a bond with a jury faster than any lawyer I have ever seen. He makes jurors like him and trust him, and in return, they like and trust his clients.*[47]

Unfortunately, there is not yet a historical marker in the city of Chattanooga that honors the life, contributions and memory of attorney Noah Walter Parden.

Bessie Smith, Empress of the Blues

The Greatest Vaudeville Blues Singer of All Time; the Most Successful African American Performing Artist of All Time

Bessie Smith was one of seven children born in poverty to African American parents in Chattanooga, Tennessee. By the time she was nine years old both of Smith's parents were dead and her older sister, Viola, was raising her. To help support the family, Smith began singing and dancing for money on the streets of Chattanooga. She was apparently very good at what she did because a club operator in Chattanooga heard her voice and quickly offered her $8 per week to sing at his tavern.

In 1912, Smith's older brother Clarence came back into Chattanooga with a show that included blues singer Ma Rainey. Clarence hired Smith as a dancer for the show, and it did not take long for Ma Rainey to take Smith on as her protégée.

By the 1920s, Smith was a leading artist in black shows on the Theater Owners Booking Agency (TOBA) circuit and at the 81 Theater in Atlanta. In 1923, her first recording—"Down Hearted Blues"—was such a success that it sold a colossal 780,000 copies. This song established Smith as the most successful African American performing artist of her time.

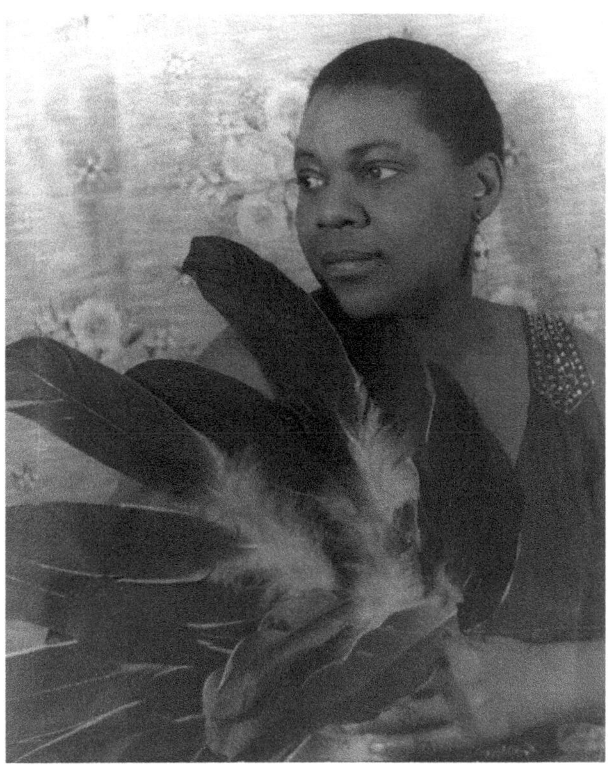

This is a photograph of Bessie Smith, famous African American blues singer from Chattanooga, Tennessee. *Photograph courtesy of the Library of Congress, Prints & Photographs Division, Carl Van Vechten Collection.*

Smith continued to record, performing with such musicians as Fletcher Henderson, Louis Armstrong, Joe Smith and James P. Johnston. She also continued to perform on the road, touring throughout the North and South and performing to large audiences. Her shows were said to be quite elaborate and typically included up to forty performers.

In 1929, Smith appeared in the seventeen-minute film *St. Louis Blues*, but by that time alcoholism had taken its toll on her career. Smith died in September 1937 while being transported down Route 61. The road was narrow and poorly lit, and Smith's driver slammed into the back of a parked truck. Smith suffered devastating injuries, including the partial amputation of one of her arms. Her death is clouded in mystery, but it is probable that she died of excessive blood loss while en route to the hospital, and not because she was turned away from a white hospital as the rumor goes.

MARY WALKER

The Oldest Student in the United States; Chattanooga's Ambassador of Goodwill

Mary (Grandma) Walker was born a slave in Union Springs, Alabama, in 1848. The details of her slave life are not easily accessible; however, research into archived newspapers and local museums continues.

Mary was only seventeen years old when emancipation came. She relocated to Chattanooga, Tennessee, in 1917 when she was sixty-nine years old, and for the next forty-seven years, she lived her life and conducted her daily affairs without the luxury of being able to read.

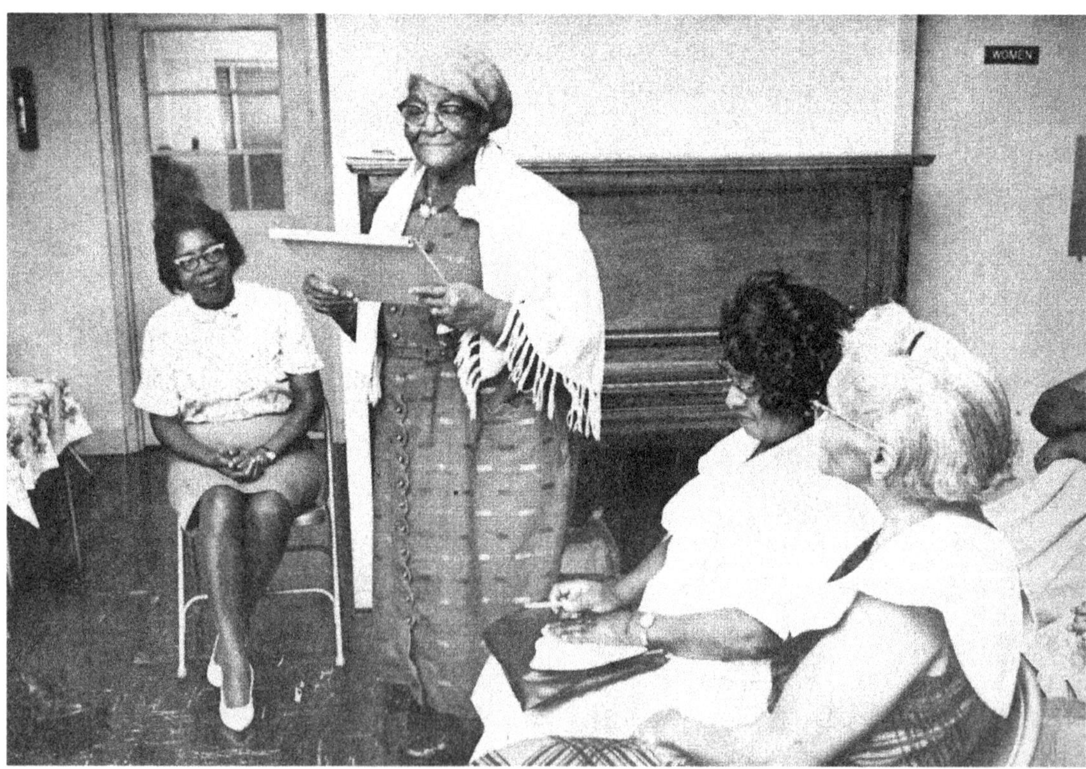

Mary "Grandma" Walker became a national celebrity when she learned to read at age 116. Aside from being declared the nation's oldest student by the United States Department of Health, Education and Welfare, she was also twice named Chattanooga's ambassador of goodwill. *Photograph courtesy of Chattanooga-Hamilton County Bicentennial Library.*

It is not known whether all those years of illiteracy finally took their toll on Mary, or whether simply being in a progressive city like Chattanooga inspired her to better herself. However, by the age of 116, Mary was finished with illiteracy. She set her goal then enrolled in a Chattanooga Area Literacy Movement (CALM) class to learn to read, write and solve basic arithmetic problems.

Mary met her goal, and her success was so singular that the United States Department of Health, Education and Welfare declared her "the nation's oldest student." Her accomplishment became a symbol of hope and inspiration to students everywhere, because the plain truth was that if a 116-year-old woman could learn to read, *anyone* could learn to read.

The City of Chattanooga was pleased with Mary's national status. Chattanooga twice bestowed on her their Ambassador of Goodwill Award.

Uncle Mark Thrash

America's Oldest Living Citizen; Nation's Oldest Voter

Uncle Mark Thrash was a nationally known figure who lived in Chickamauga-Chattanooga National Military Park (Chickamauga Battlefield) and entertained tourists from all over the United States. He told stories about his part in the Civil War, and how he made muskets for the Union Soldiers. He lived until the ripe old age of "almost 123," and died eight days before his 123rd birthday. He was married five times, and had twenty-nine children. He was the patient of Dr. W. Alexander Thompson, a Chattanooga African American physician, and he was friend to many of the elderly ex-slaves living in the Chattanooga area.

Uncle Mark and his twin brother Mark Anthony were born in a little log cabin on December 25, 1820. The cabin was located in Richmond, Virginia, and belonged to Dr. Christopher Thrash—who was actually a preacher and not a physician. Uncle Mark's parents were both from Jamaica and had only been living in the United States as slaves for six months at the time the twins were born. They had had at least ten other children when they were in Jamaica, but for some reason or other these children were left behind for the other slave traders to haggle over.

When Uncle Mark was twenty years old, Dr. Thrash paid ten cents an acre for five hundred acres of land that he purchased from American Indians near Griffith, Georgia. Dr. Thrash sent Uncle Mark, Mark Anthony, their parents and several other slaves to help clear and settle the new property. When the slaves arrived, the Native Americans gave them an all-day picnic not unlike the first picnic that the American Indians gave to the Pilgrims. This was the Native Americans' way of welcoming these slaves to the area, and the feast came complete with wild game, vegetables and other delicacies.

Uncle Mark's white apron was the stuff of legends. As one story went, Dr. Thrash owned so many slaves in those days that he could not distinguish his own from those on the neighboring plantation, so he commanded his slaves to wear white aprons over their clothes to make them distinguishable. Another story

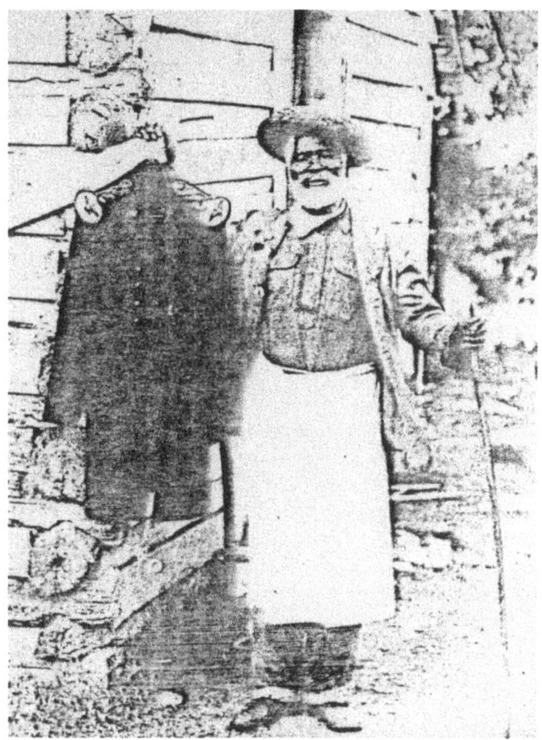

A very faded photograph of Uncle Mark Thrash, who lived on the Chickamauga Battlefield. Uncle Mark fought in the Battle Above the Clouds, and was the nation's oldest citizen and the world's oldest twin. He was a veteran of both the Union and Confederate armies, and had many close friends in Chattanooga, including Dr. W. Alexander Thompson, a Chattanooga physician. *Photograph courtesy of the Chickamauga and Chattanooga National Military Park.*

quoted Uncle Mark as saying that the white aprons were distributed to distinguish house slaves from field slaves, and since Uncle Mark was a house slave, it was only fitting that he wear one.

By the time the Civil War was in full swing, Uncle Mark was already forty-one years old and had many children of his own. He was captured by some of the Civil War forces and sent to Florida, but he was soon returned to the Thrash plantation near Griffith because he was considered too old to fight. By the time he returned to the plantation, he discovered that one of his master's sons and his own eldest son had disappeared. Both Uncle Mark and Dr. Thrash were afraid their sons had been forced to serve at the Battle of Chickamauga, and Dr. Thrash encouraged Uncle Mark to travel to Chickamauga, Georgia, in search of the boys.

Uncle Mark arrived at Chickamauga barely three days after the bloody battle. He claimed that what he saw and smelled at the Chickamauga battlefield was enough to convince him that no man could live through such carnage. The battlefield was littered with the bodies of thousands of dead soldiers—approximately thirty-six thousand, in fact—and they were all bloated and flyblown. There were also thousands of decaying horses, mules and cattle. Uncle Mark described the air as being "full of obnoxious odors." He said:

> *Really, I didn't think the breeze would ever clear up so folks could live. But we got busy burying the dead, and in about 15 days, conditions became bearable.*[48]

While performing the gruesome tasks at Chickamauga, Uncle Mark met President Garfield, who was a major general in the Union Army at the time. He claimed that the future president Garfield jokingly ordered him "not to bury the Blues together with the Grays because they might come to life and start fighting the battle all over again."[49]

Aside from working under future president Garfield, Uncle Mark served as an orderly for General Stewart, General Boyton, General Carmack and many other officials.

Uncle Mark finally located his own son and the son of Dr. Thrash. Once he knew the boys were alive and well, he decided to travel a bit as a free man. He drifted to Memphis, Tennessee, but soon suffered an attack of malaria. He then returned to North Georgia and began living on the Chickamauga Battlefield, and there he lived for the remainder of his life.

When Uncle Mark had first arrived on the Chickamauga Battlefield it was only a field of horror with thousands of rotting corpses that were in need of burial. But by the time he died in 1943, that bloody place was rechristened the Chickamauga Military National Park and had been transformed into one of the most beautiful spots in the area. Uncle Mark claimed that he helped to erect practically every monument in the Chickamauga Park, and even helped lay every foot of road there.

In his long lifetime, Uncle Mark fathered twenty-nine children. In one interview, he admitted that he had so many children that he sometimes forgot their names. At the time of his death, he was survived by his fifth wife, eighteen of his twenty-nine children, ten grandchildren and two of his seventeen great-great grandchildren.

Uncle Mark attracted worldwide attention several times in his lifetime. He attracted attention when he married his fifth wife at the age of 107. During World War I, he created quite a stir when he wrote to President Woodrow Wilson and requested permission to accompany one of the Fort Oglethorpe commanders to France. President Wilson reportedly denied the brave request, stating that Uncle Mark had already done his part, and that "the younger folks could fight this war."[50]

Another time in 1913, Uncle Mark created a stir when the United States government had to retire him from his work at the Chickamauga Park at the age of 103. They had not realized he was so old. Actually, the government was used to people who applied for a pension so they didn't have to work, but Uncle Mark had cheerfully continued his work in the battlefield without argument or complaint. He might have continued that way if his former master's oldest son had not sent the government a crumpled page from the Thrash family bible with Uncle Mark's 1820 birth date scribbled in the pages. After government officials got over their initial shock, they quickly gave Uncle Mark his well-deserved pension.

Yet another time, Uncle Mark attracted worldwide attention when he and his twin brother, Mark Anthony, reunited for the first time in years—at the age of 117. The brothers met in Chattanooga, Tennessee, in September 1938, the seventy-fifth anniversary of the Battle Above the Clouds, and when they did, they were christened the world's oldest living twins.

Uncle Mark achieved much fame in his long lifetime. Tourists came from all over the country to talk with him and listen to his colorful stories about the Civil War.

Teachers brought their students to the Chickamauga Park for hands-on field trips. In addition, Uncle Mark was invited to speak on "We the People," a program carried by the Columbia Broadcast System, in 1937, 1939 and 1943. He talked about his experiences in the Civil War, and was also often asked about his first impressions of the telephone, airplane, radio and car, because he was born before any of these necessities existed and was still around when each was invented.

Uncle Mark was the subject of a book called *Seen the Glory: The Story of the Oldest Person of our Country, 1820–1943*, by Stephen O. Addison, and was also featured on the debut cover of *Shades of Greatness: A Calendar Tribute to Early African American Inventors* by the author Rita Lorraine Hubbard. He has also been the subject of many college papers and treatments.

Uncle Mark died on December 18, 1943, just eight days short of his 123rd birthday. Approximately six hundred people of both races gathered at the Friendship Baptist Church to say goodbye to him. He was laid to rest wearing his ceremonial apron over his clothing. Among the speakers at his funeral were Dr. W. Alexander Thompson, an elk physician and one of Chattanooga's early African American physicians, and Professor W.J. Davenport, then principal of Howard High School.

Uncle Mark was given a military funeral, which in 1943 was the first time ever that a civilian was given such a funeral in the Chickamauga Georgia/Hamilton County area. He was laid to rest in a portion of the old Haslerig cemetery. His grave was decorated with an unmarked stone for forty years. Finally, in 1982, Chickamauga Park historian Edward Tinney helped to raise funds to place a headstone on Uncle Mark's resting place.

Uncle Mark Set Records:
Country's Oldest Living Citizen
Country's Oldest Voter
Country's Oldest Civil War Pensioner
World's Oldest Living Twin

Captain Morris B. Glen

First African American to Rise to the Position of Captain of Police in a Major Southern City

Captain Morris Glenn was one of the first African Americans to serve on Chattanooga's police force in the mid-1900s. He was also the first male of his race to rise to the position of captain of police in the entire South.

Morris Bertram Glenn was a native of Athens, Georgia, but was orphaned at an early age and had to be raised by relatives who lived in Chattanooga. He spent his early years at West Main Street Elementary School. Later he enrolled at Howard High School, where he played football before enlisting in the army to fight in World War II.

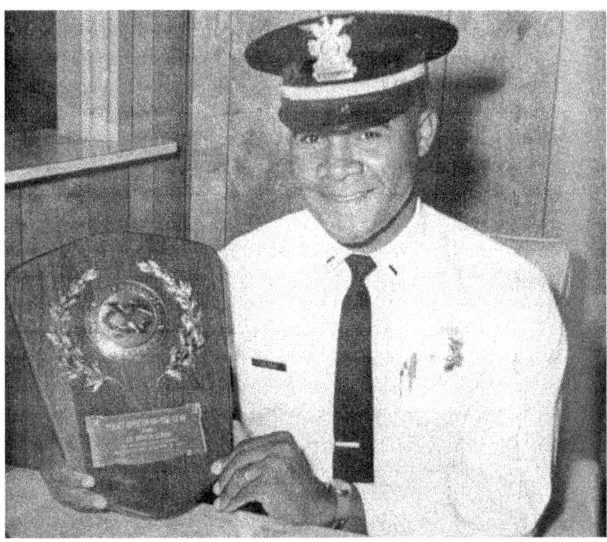

A 1967 photograph of a smiling Lieutenant Morris Glenn proudly displaying his Officer of the Year award. *Photograph courtesy of the* Centurion: A History of the Chattanooga Police Department, 1852–1977

Glenn's tour of duty lasted three years. He was a member of a combat engineer's unit that was stationed first in North Africa, and later with invasion forces in Corsica, Sicily, Italy and France.

When his tour of duty was over, Glenn returned to Chattanooga and worked for the Tennessee Valley Authority (TVA) for three years. Later he was accepted into the Chattanooga Police Department under the late police commissioner Roy Hyatt.

Glenn's first assignment was walking a beat on East 9th Street. He spent fourteen and a half years in that position, and developed his own philosophy about policing. "I would rather make peace," he said, "than have to bang somebody around. I want to be fair to everybody."[51]

At the end of the fourteen and a half years Glenn was finally promoted to sergeant by former commissioner Herbert P. Dunlap. After that he advanced quickly, winning his lieutenant's bars after only two years as a sergeant and winning his captain's status two years later in 1968.

During his career, Captain Morris Glenn proved himself to be an outstanding policeman. He received many citations and awards, including the National Exchange Club Policeman of the Year Award. Even then governor George Wallace was impressed with Captain Glenn. Wallace was making an attempt for the presidency, and his campaign trail brought him to Chattanooga. Captain Glenn provided excellent police protection for Wallace, and he was so impressed that he wrote to thank him for his services.

Unfortunately, Captain Glenn would enjoy his tenure as captain for only three years. On the night of March 20, 1971, he was en route to south Chattanooga to investigate a shooting when he was involved in a car accident. He had activated both his lights and his siren, yet a civilian car still pulled out in front of him. Glenn swerved to miss the car, but was struck broadside by another vehicle. He suffered back and internal injuries.

At first it looked as if Glenn would survive, and doctors listed his condition as fair. But after eighteen days in the hospital, Captain Glenn suffered "complications" from his injuries and died on April 7, 1971.

At the time of his death, Captain Glenn had been the sole remaining active member of Chattanooga's first contingent of African American officers, who had been sworn in on June 10, 1948.

5.

Notable Places and Events That Had an Impact on the United States

Integration of Chattanooga Police Force

One of the First Southern Cities to Integrate its Police Force

On August 11, 1948, the first seven African American police officers to serve the city of Chattanooga, Tennessee, since the year 1883 went on duty. At 3:30 p.m. on that day, Morris Glenn, Arthur Heard, C.E. Black, W.B. Baulridge, Singer Askins, Thomas Patterson and Thaddeus Arnold were sworn in for active duty by city judge Riley Graham.

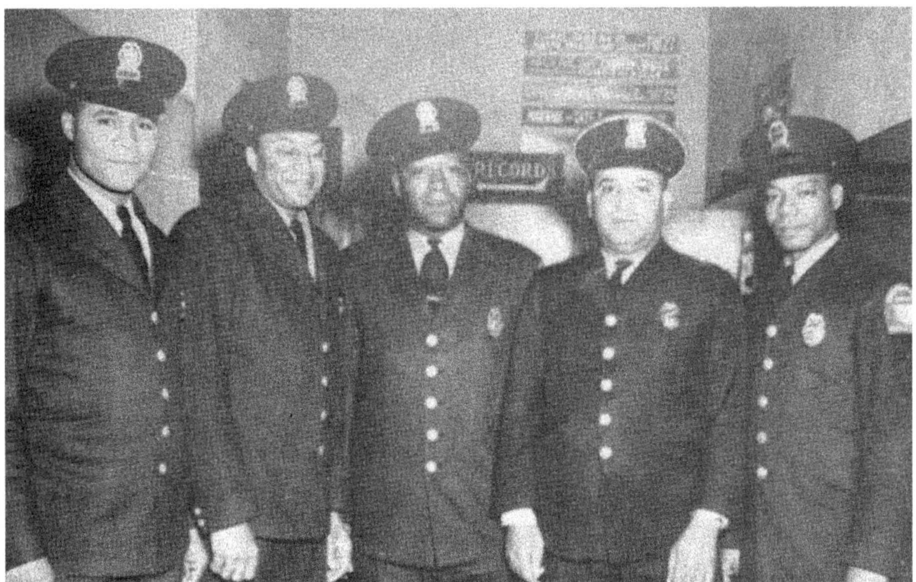

On August 11, 1948, the first African American police officers to serve the city of Chattanooga since the year 1883 went on duty. They were, from left to right: Officers Morris Glenn, Arthur Heard, C.E. Black, W.B. Baulridge and Singer Askins. Not shown were: Thomas Patterson and Thaddeus Arnold. *Photograph courtesy of the Centurion, 1852–1977.*

Within the next half hour, the men had already taken up their "walking beats" on East 9th Street. Of course segregation was still alive and well in the general population, so these officers were not permitted to arrest white citizens. Rather, they were restricted to walking beats in black neighborhoods.

Still, this momentous occasion propelled Chattanooga to the front of the line as one of the first Southern cities to integrate its police force. Black and white community leaders, family and friends attended the ceremonies, which marked one giant step forward for equality and integration.

The Martin Hotel

Largest African American Hotel in the South

The Martin Hotel was at one time hailed as the largest African American hotel in the entire South and kindly accommodated the big names in African American entertainment when stark racism kept many stars from registering at white hotels.

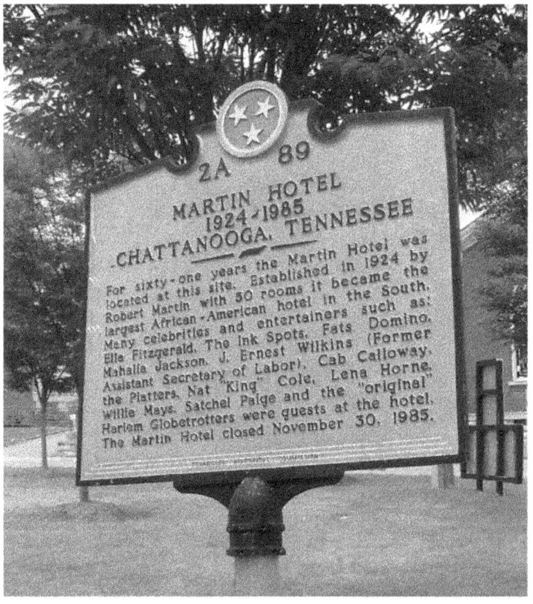

This is a photograph of the historical marker that commemorates the Martin Hotel. The Martin once served as host for such famous African Americans as Ella Fitzgerald, Fats Domino, The Ink Spots, Mahalia Jackson, Lena Horne and Nat King Cole. The marker is located at 215 West M.L. King Blvd. (formerly West 9th Street) in front of the Bessie Smith Hall. *Photograph courtesy of Rita Lorraine Hubbard, ©2004.*

Established by Mr. Robert Martin in 1924, The Martin Hotel's impressive fifty rooms were more than spacious enough to accommodate such names as Mahalia Jackson, the Ink Spots, Ella Fitzgerald, Fats Domino, Lena Horne and Nat King Cole. Other famous visitors included Cab Calloway, The Platters, Willie Mays, Satchel Paige, and the original Harlem Globetrotters. Once, even assistant secretary of labor J. Ernest Wilkins took a room at the Martin Hotel.

The Martin Hotel was located on 9th Street (currently M.L. King Boulevard), in front of the present-day Bessie Smith Hall and the African American History Museum. The Martin Hotel historical marker is all that remains of this important landmark.

Haslerig Dairy

Only African American Owned Dairy of its Type in the South

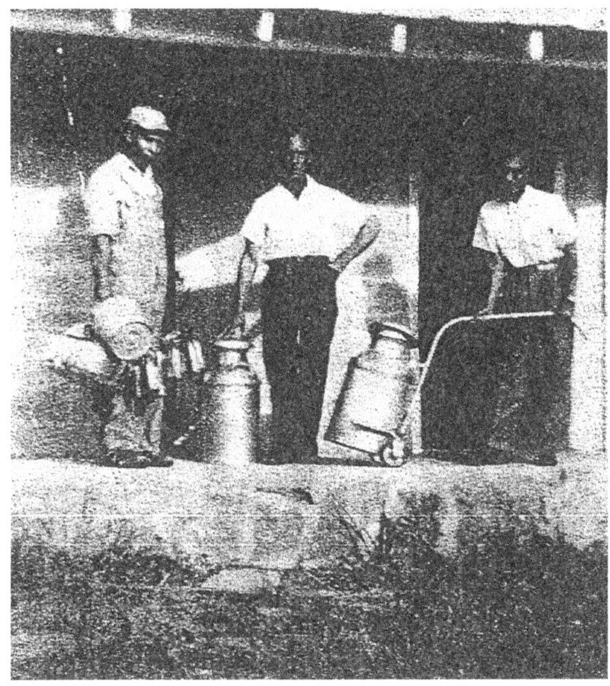

An early photograph of some workers at the Haslerig Dairy Farm, date unknown. *Photograph courtesy of Rod Morton.*

In the early 1900s, an African American man named C.D. Haslerig ran a general farm where he milked cows, raised a flock of chickens and tended a large vegetable garden. Haslerig's efforts paid off, and he soon found that he had quite a bit of surplus. Since his family could never hope to consume all that he farmed, this early entrepreneur began to peddle his excess—milk, eggs, butter and vegetables, to other families.

By the spring of 1949, Haslerig had established an impressive customer base. He delivered his dairy products and vegetables door-to-door, and his customers welcomed his fresh produce with open arms. Then, because food regulations and restrictions were being developed and enforced across the United States, Haslerig applied for a milk processing permit with the City of Chattanooga's health department. He also decided to build a processing plant, which would be equipped with the best and most modern equipment of that time and would be located in Chickamauga, Georgia.

Haslerig's slogan was: "From the Farm to You."[52] The Haslerig Dairy was said to be the only African American dairy of its type in the entire South.

Haslerig's business, which had begun with one delivery truck, soon grew in size until he operated five refrigerated delivery trucks and one transport truck. At one time, Haslerig Farm supplied all the milk for the "colored" schools of the city. In other words, an entire generation of African Americans grew up on Haslerig's milk.

In 1957, C.D. Haslerig died, leaving his sons Charles and Willie to carry on the family business. But by the early 1960s, the cost of operation was too much to bear. Everything seemed to be going up in price: Labor costs, machinery costs, raw materials and utilities! The larger dairy companies might have no problems with such rising costs, but the Haslerig Dairy simply couldn't keep up. The dairy closed in the mid-1960s.

The James and Allen Drug Company

One of the Largest African American–Owned Drugstores in the United States

The James and Allen Drug Company was owned by Dr. O.W. James and Mr. Allen. This company furnished prescription drugs to the East Side Pharmacy, which at one time was considered the finest black owned pharmacy in the United States.

Both the James and Allen Drug Company and the East Side Pharmacy were located inside the James Building. The James Building was once located on East 9th Street, and was considered one of the most modern facilities of its time. It had ample office space and rooms for lodging, and had "all the necessary sanitary arrangements." Like many other fine structures at the turn of the century, the James Building was built entirely by African American labor.

Lincoln Park

First Lighted Softball Fields for African Americans in the South

Lincoln Park was at one time the only recreational facility for African Americans in all of Chattanooga. But even more importantly, Lincoln Park had the first lighted softball fields for African Americans in the entire South. Before Lincoln Park came into existence, African American sports were consigned to the darkness after the sun

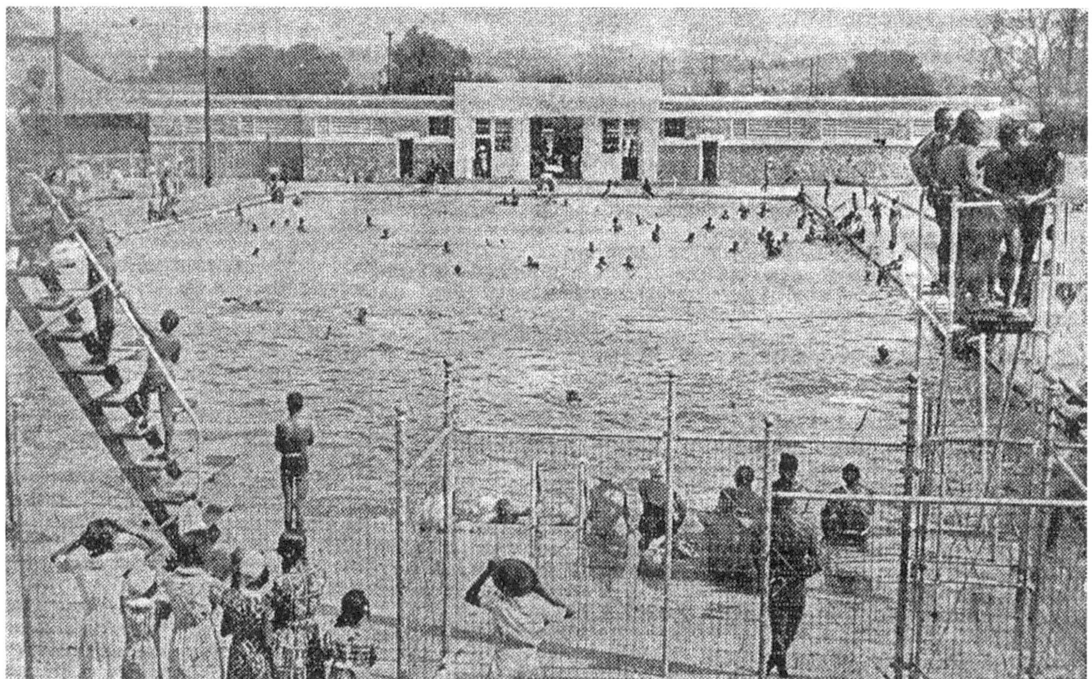

New Negro Swimming Pool at Lincoln Park: This classic photograph appeared in the *Chattanooga Times* in September 1938 and boasted about the sixty thousand dollar price tag of what was said to be "the finest pool for Negroes in the South."

went down. But once Lincoln Park opened, African American teams came from all over the South to use the facilities. In fact, more than thirty teams used its facilities. Because its fields were lighted, the teams could use the facilities day and night.

On September 18, 1938, the Lincoln Park swimming pool made its debut. This new pool cost $60,000 and was said to be the finest pool for Negroes anywhere in the entire South.

Part III

Early Medical Care

When we sit down at set of sun
To count the things that we have done,
and counting, find one self-denying act,
one word that eased the heart of him who heard,
One glance most kind, that fell like sunshine where it went,
Then we may count that day well spent.

—*Excerpt from "Forty Years a Cook," by Lula Rogers in* Chattanooga Times, *December 15, 1935.*

6.

Early Medical Care in Chattanooga

The one occupation that was grossly underrepresented in the early years of Chattanooga's African American development was the field of medicine.

In Chattanooga's early years there were only six practicing physicians—all white—which included Dr. Milo Smith, Dr. Philander Sims and Dr. W.E. Kennedy.[53] African American doctors were unheard of, and indeed, African American men who called themselves doctors were laughed at and considered a vulgar joke. Only midwives and medicine men served the early African American community, but typical of the times, their names were not important enough to be recorded in documents of any importance in the early years.

But at last in the late 1870s, Chattanooga made small strides in African American medical care. Dr. G.W. Macker, a handsome young African American male, graduated from Meharry Medical College and set up a dental practice in 1878. Originally from Spartanburg, North Carolina, Dr. Macker had once been a traveling teacher offering instruction in decorative painting and artwork. He eventually became one of Chattanooga's leading dentists in the African American community.[54]

About that same time in 1878, Dr. Thomas William Haigler hung his proud shingle in Chattanooga—and not a moment too soon, because the Negro population was exploding. Back during the November 7, 1865, census, there had been 900 Negro males, 930 Negro females and 827 Negro children in Chattanooga proper. But another 3,500 or so Negroes lived across the Tennessee River and all along its banks in the shanties and tents of Contraband town—later known as North Chattanooga.[55] Like other contraband had done all across the South, these Negro vagrants had decided to follow the Federal soldiers as they marched across the cities that they had conquered. This particular group of Negroes had drifted into Chattanooga with the Negro soldiers who would build Chattanooga's National Cemetery to bury the Civil War dead, and they had never left.

The dashing Dr. Haigler was already twenty-five years old when he settled in Chattanooga. Originally from South Carolina, he was a versatile thinker, and Chattanooga African Americans considered him to be one of the brilliant men of

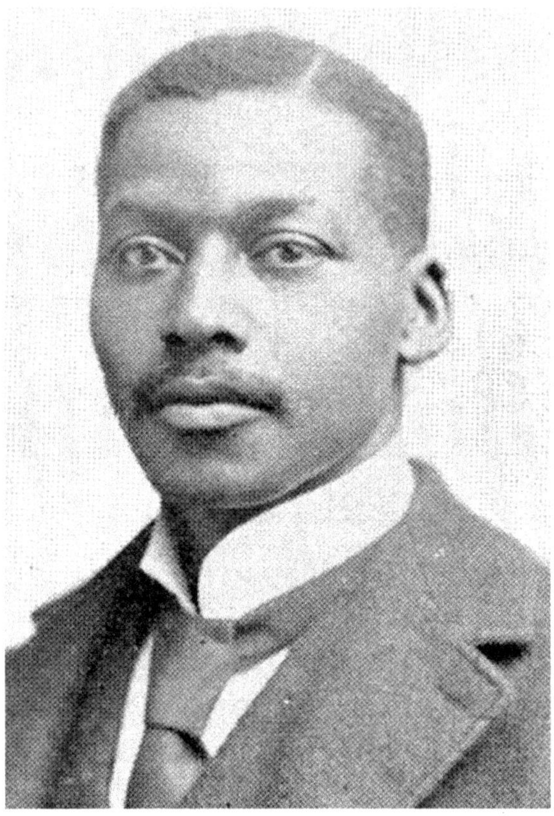

Dr. G.W. Macker, an 1898 graduate of Meharry Medical College. He became one of Chattanooga's leading dentists. *Photograph courtesy of* 1904 Biography and Achievements of the Colored Citizens of Chattanooga *by J. Bliss White.*

his time. He arrived just as the yellow fever epidemic moved into full swing and the community was grateful to have him.

The Negro census had by this time, climbed to near 7,399,[56] even after the deadly toll of the yellow fever, and all of these unfortunate souls had been living completely without medical resources. They were thrilled to be getting such a fine specimen as Dr. Haigler, who had graduated from the Louisville National Medical College with high honors as a doctor of medicine and surgery. He offered the Chattanooga Negroes good service as a general practitioner, a surgeon, a pharmacist and a mesmerizing orator, and quickly captivated them with his busy hands, his tireless demeanor and his impossibly witty brain. In fact, it was often related that he was "a man without a single lazy bone in his body."[57]

Though progress was definitely slow, the city did continue to make medical strides. By 1898, Dr. Haigler had established a unique little medical college for Negroes called the Chattanooga National Medical College. He trained individuals in the medical field and did such an excellent job of it that the college became quite well known in the region.[58]

CHATTANOOGA NEGROES AND CITY HOSPITALS

In Chattanooga in 1860 there were 457 Negroes, of which 93 were "free," and the closest they got to a hospital was when a "force"—or large group of them—was put to work cleaning out the old buildings that were to be used for the 1,200 or so sick and convalescent Confederate soldiers, plucked fresh from the Civil War battlefield, who were being evacuated from Nashville.[59] Other than this, no one—Negro or white—had ever heard of hospitals.

In 1871, the word "hospital" was still virtually unknown. When a distraught young white man attempted to commit suicide in an empty house, the owner of the home had no clue what to do about him—proof that there was nothing resembling a hospital in the city during that time. The homeowner persuaded some of the area youth to hold a night vigil over the man's unconscious body, and they agreed, passing the time away singing and laughing and playing games while they waited to see if the poor man would live. He eventually recovered.

By 1875, a year before Meharry Medical College was established in Nashville, Tennessee, Chattanooga had a semblance of a "hospital" on record. It was a dismal, dreaded place attended by "an old medical gentleman," and targeted as the final destination for the very poor, the very destitute and those sickly Negroes with highly infectious diseases. The building was rickety and brooding—a lopsided wooden contraption that had been used for some purpose or other during the Civil War and that, to be honest, no one in their right mind thought of as a place for healing. It was merely a holding place to isolate the infectious, the unbearable and the unwanted of society, who were hoarded inside to wait to meet their medical fate.

In 1891, the cornerstone was laid for the Baroness Erlanger Hospital, and by 1899 the West Building of Erlanger was ready for use by the patients, while the East Building would house the nurses and other hospital workers. As the legend went, a ward on the ground floor and far off to the rear of the West Building entrance was said to be designated for Negro men, while the very top floor of the same building was said to be designated for Negro women.[60]

In 1902, Dr. George West teamed with Dr. G. Manning Ellis, another white physician, and together they purchased the old John L. Divine home, located at 612 West 9th Street. With this property, they opened what they called the West-Ellis Hospital, a private hospital for Chattanooga's white citizens.[61] Of course, West-Ellis Hospital would add twelve rooms in 1906, and in 1910, the doctors would benevolently add a large wood frame structure that would serve as a "colored department" to insure appropriate separation of Negroes from whites. This small medical development—still a few years away—would let a tiny ray of light shine through the solid stone of southern medical discrimination…but only a tiny bit. For the most part, though, Chattanooga's hospitals were still in the early stages of growth, and adequate healthcare facilities for Negroes seemed to be the last item on the city agenda.

Early healthcare in Chattanooga was a horrendous affair, especially among African Americans. Their conditions were unsanitary, and poor health and high mortality rates plagued the African American community. Tuberculosis cases roared through the community, yet the acutely ill and the chronically ill who needed healthcare were promptly directed to the basements of existing white hospitals to receive their care. African American doctors had little or no admitting privileges in area hospitals like Erlanger Hospital.

Walden Hospital

In 1915, Walden Hospital became Chattanooga's first and only African American teaching hospital. When its doors opened to Chattanooga's African American population, nothing like it had ever been seen in Chattanooga before...and nothing like it had ever been done for Chattanooga's Negroes.

But before giving further description of Walden Hospital, perhaps a bit of background should be given on early African American physicians in Chattanooga.

7.

Early African American Physicians

The following names and biographies of early physicians are largely taken from the book *Biography and Achievements of the Colored Citizens of Chattanooga, 1904*, by J. Bliss White. Not featured are the biographies and achievements of Dr. O.W. James, Dr. Callier or Dr. Patton. It is known that these physicians were in practice during the early 1900s, because Dr. James's name is mentioned in White's 1904 book. Also, a close inspection of the 1914 photograph of Walden Hospital reveals office signs for both Dr. Callier and Dr. Patton.

Unfortunately, information about their lives and practices has not been as easily accessed as those included in the White book. Therefore, any omission of early African American physicians from this volume is not intentional. Subsequent biographies will be noted in later volumes.

Dr. O.L. Davis

First and Only African American Female Dentist to Graduate in the South

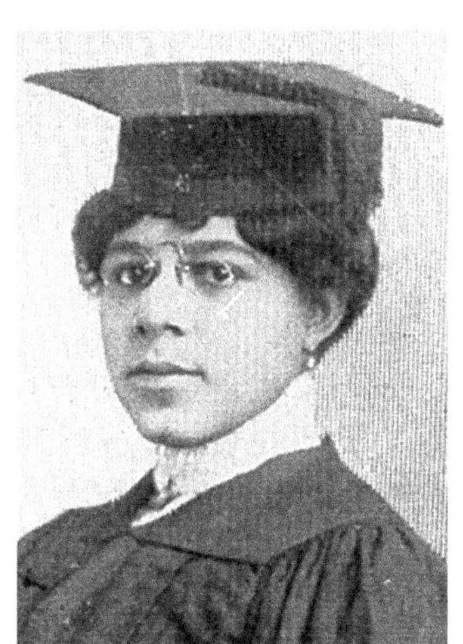

Dr. O.L. Davis was a prominent figure in Chattanooga, and practiced dentistry in the James Building. She was born in Hamilton County, Tennessee, on Old Lookout Mountain, and attended public schools in Chattanooga. Later she attended Spellman Seminary in Atlanta, Georgia. She finished her dentistry degree at Meharry Medical College in 1902.

In 1904, Dr. O.L. Davis was the first and only "colored" female dentist to graduate in the South in 1904, and the first to enter the practice. Her practice was located in the James Building on East 9th Street. *Photograph courtesy of* 1904 Biography and Achievements of the Colored Citizens of Chattanooga *by J. Bliss White.*

By 1904 Dr. Davis was the first and only colored female dentist to graduate in the South, and the first to enter the practice. Her practice was located in the James Building on East 9th Street (now named M.L. King Boulevard.)

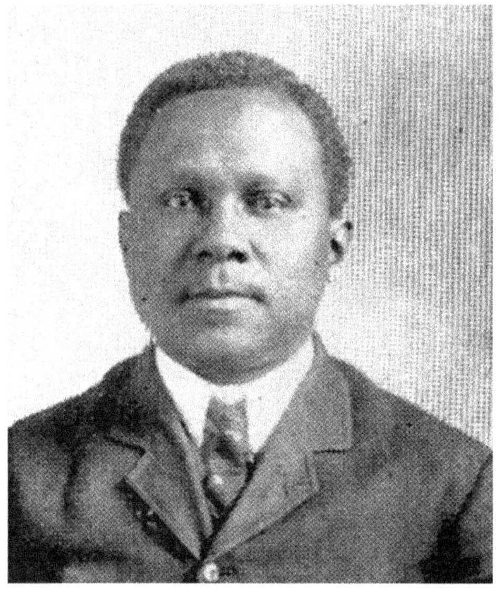

DR. WILLIAM H. ELMORE

Dr. William H. Elmore was born on May 16, 1862, and had the misfortune of becoming an orphan at a very young age. He was raised in Augusta, Georgia, and studied dentistry there and at Nashville, Tennessee. Dr. Elmore came to Chattanooga in 1887 and set up practice at 108 ½ Market Street. His home was located at 510 Carolina Street in Highland Park.

This is an early photograph of Dr. William H. Elmore, whose medical practice was located at 401 West 9th Street. *Photograph courtesy of* 1904 Biography and Achievements of the Colored Citizens of Chattanooga *by J. Bliss White.*

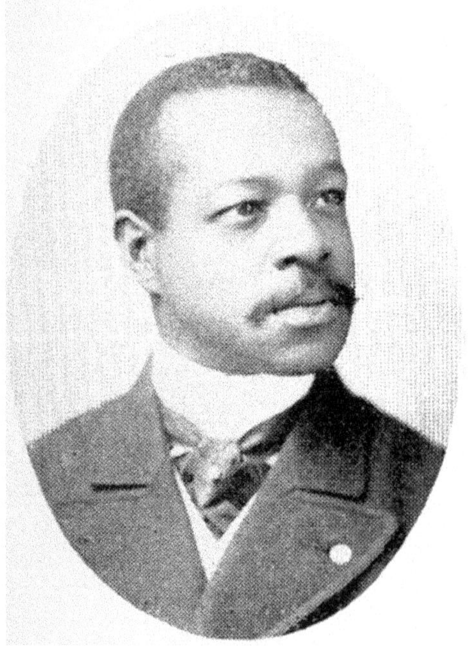

DR. J.P. FRIERSON

Dr. J.P. Frierson was born in Murfreesboro, Tennessee, on April 14, 1871. After attending public schools in Columbia, Tennessee, he came to Chattanooga in 1890. He pursued a dental career at Meharry Medical College in Nashville, and finished his courses as valedictorian of his class in 1903. He returned to Chattanooga soon after, and set up his dental practice in an office on Market Street.

Dr. Frierson is credited with having some of the more up-to-date knowledge of dental procedures of 1904.

Dr. J.P. Frierson was an early Chattanooga dentist who was credited with having up-to-date knowledge of dental procedures. *Photograph courtesy of* 1904 Biography and Achievements of the Colored Citizens of Chattanooga *by J. Bliss White.*

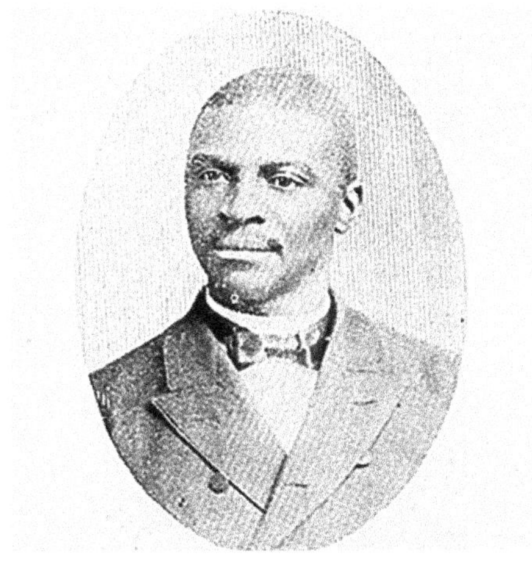

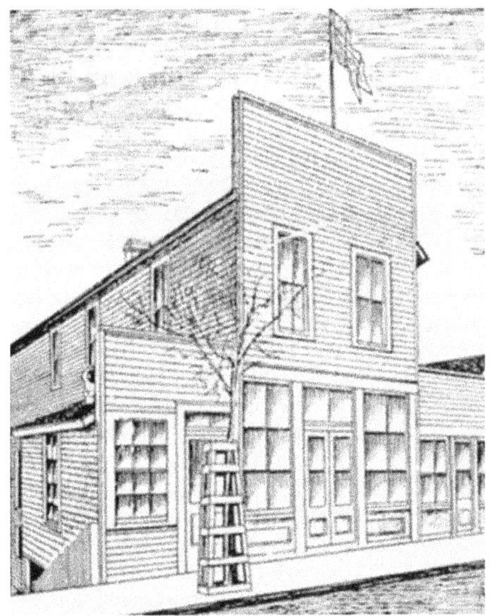

Dr. Thomas William Haigler

Dr. Thomas William Haigler was a physician, surgeon, pharmacist and orator. He was also founder of the Chattanooga National Medical College.

Born in Orangeburg County, South Carolina, on July 4, 1857, to a farmer and a seamstress, Thomas Haigler received a common education. After he graduated from school, he soon left the farm life to pursue studies as a schoolteacher, chopping wood and painting furniture to help pay for his college education.

Haigler's studies included the classics at Claflin University in South Carolina, business at Clark University in Atlanta, theology at Gammon School in Atlanta, philosophy in Chicago, pharmacy at Northwestern University in Ohio, stenography in Toledo and medicine at Northwestern Medical College, Toledo Medical College and Meharry Medical College.

With such an outstanding educational background to precede him, Haigler graduated from Louisville National Medical College with high honors as doctor of medicine and surgery. In 1878, Dr. Haigler hung his shingle in Chattanooga, Tennessee, setting up his practice as physician and surgeon. In 1890, Haigler opened his own drugstore. And on October 3, 1898, he organized the Chattanooga National Medical College, and trained many promising individuals.

In Dr. Haigler's day, it was often said of him: "There is not a lazy bone in the man."

He was considered a natural born leader and had several mottos, such as "Grit, grace and greenbacks," which he interpreted as being religion for the soul, education for the head and money for the pocket.

Top: Dr. Thomas William Haigler was one of the most versatile and intelligent African Americans of Chattanooga. He was a physician, surgeon, pharmacist and orator, and was founder of the Chattanooga National Medical College. His motto was "Grit, grace and greenbacks," meaning religion for the soul, education for the head and money for the pocket. *Photograph courtesy of* 1904 Biography and Achievements of the Colored Citizens of Chattanooga *by J. Bliss White.*

Bottom: This is an early drawing of the Chattanooga National Medical College, which was organized by Dr. Thomas William Haigler on October 3, 1898. Dr. Haigler trained many promising individuals at this college. *Image courtesy of* 1904 Biography and Achievements of the Colored Citizens of Chattanooga *by J. Bliss White.*

DR. EDMOND W. ROGERS

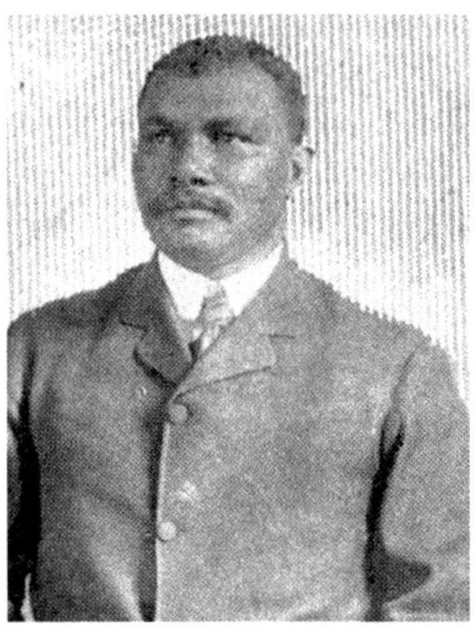

Edmond W. Rogers was born in Mississippi in 1868. He left his parents at the age of thirteen and worked at railroad building, steam milling and other hard labor for the next seven years. He did not enter public school until age twenty-one, and once he completed his studies, he taught in various county schools. He later pursued more schooling, eventually graduating from Meharry Medical College in 1901. He quickly located in Chattanooga and set up his practice on April 1, 1901.

His office was located at 211½ East 9th Street, and his practice was described as "phenomenal."

A 1904 photograph of Dr. Edmond W. Rogers, whose practice was located at 211½ East 9th Street. Dr. Rogers began his working career as a railroad builder, turpentine maker and steam miller. When he eventually opened his medical practice in Chattanooga in 1901, he was called "a phenomenal man." *Photograph courtesy of* 1904 Biography and Achievements of the Colored Citizens of Chattanooga *by J. Bliss White.*

DR. W. ALEXANDER THOMPSON

Dr. W. Alexander Thompson was born in Shelbyville, Tennessee, on February 15, 1870. His parents, Calvin J. and Lucy Thompson, believed very strongly in educating their children. His father was one of the prime figures behind the establishment of the first public schools for black youth in Bedford County, Tennessee.

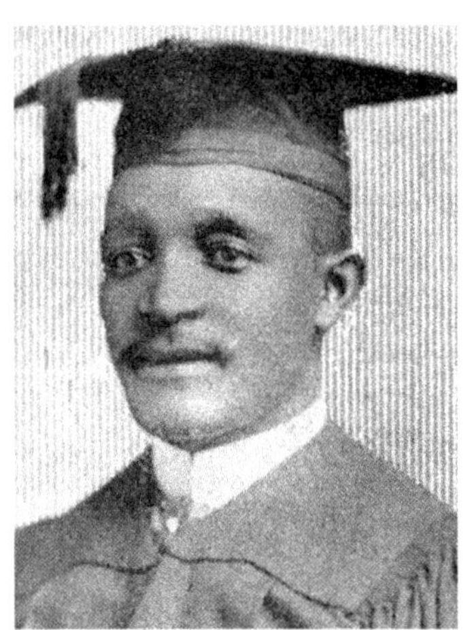

Dr. Thompson graduated from Turner High School in 1890, and the college department of Roger-Williams University in 1897. He entered Meharry Medical College immediately afterward and graduated with the class of 1903.

Dr. Thompson was the personal physician of Uncle Mark Thrash, the 123-year-old ex-slave who lived in the Chickamauga-Chattanooga National Military Park. He was also one of the speakers at Uncle Mark's funeral.

Dr. Thompson's medical practice was located at 401 West 9th Street.

Dr. W. Alexander Thompson, who began his medical practice in Chattanooga in 1903. Dr. Thompson was the personal physician of Uncle Mark Thrash, who lived on the Chickamauga Battlefield. *Photograph courtesy of* 1904 Biography and Achievements of the Colored Citizens of Chattanooga *by J. Bliss White.*

Dr. G.W. Macker

See page 86 for photograph.

Dr. G.W. Macker was born in Spartanburg, North Carolina. He taught school there for awhile then began to travel and teach decorative painting and artwork. He entered Meharry Medical College in the fall of 1895 and graduated from the dental department with the class of 1898. He began practicing dentistry in Chattanooga around 1898 and was one of the leading dentists of the city.

Dr. Emma Rochelle Wheeler

Chattanooga's First African American Female Physician

Dr. Emma Rochelle Wheeler was Chattanooga's first African American female physician—and the only one for the next thirty-five years. Dr. Wheeler was not a native Chattanoogan, but African Americans in Chattanooga, Tennessee, came to consider her one of their own.

Emma Rochelle was born near Gainesville, Florida, on February 8, 1882. Her father was a farmer and veterinarian. Emma became interested in medicine at the very tender age of six, when her father took her to see a white female doctor for a minor eye problem.

After graduating from Meharry Medical College in Nashville, Tennessee, Emma married Dr. John N. Wheeler, and she and her husband moved to Chattanooga and began practicing medicine together. When they arrived in Chattanooga fresh from their honeymoon, the Negro population had already topped 13,122—and would reach 17,942 by 1910.[62] There were at least four other doctors and three dentists listed in the city directory at the time that Emma and her husband arrived.[63]

Of course, Emma was the first African American female physician that anyone in Chattanooga—Negro or white—had ever seen, and she was indeed an oddity to the people. Unless they counted the "grannies"—the Negro midwives who delivered the babies and tried to cure the general ailments that plagued the community—there wasn't another African American lady physician like her for miles. In fact, aside from Miss Georgia Ester Lee Patton, who had earned her medical degree from Meharry in 1893 and set up her practice in Memphis—and who Chattanooga Negroes had probably never even heard of—Emma was the only African American female physician for miles in any direction.

Most of the African American physicians were centered in the downtown area, on Market Street or East 9th Street. But Wheeler and her husband chose to open their offices on Main Street. As a central location, Main Street was close enough to the downtown area for the Wheelers to be within reach of the medical community when they needed to be, yet it was also located close to several Negro communities concentrated in and around Washington Street, 16th Street, Rossville Boulevard, East End (Central Avenue) and Reed Avenue. It was also within buggy distance of the local train depot.

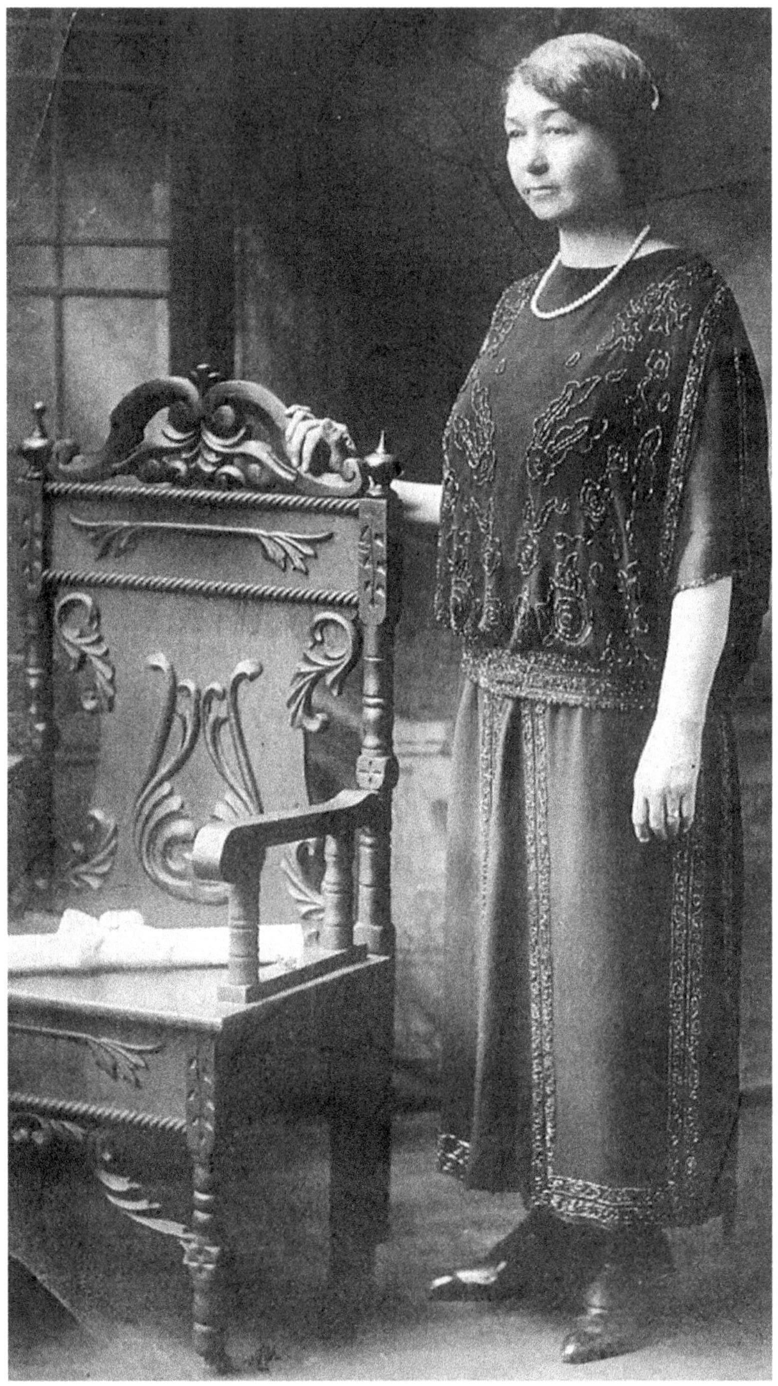

A photograph of Dr. Emma Rochelle Wheeler, graduating from Meharry Medical College in 1905. Emma would go on to found and manage Walden Hospital, Chattanooga's first and only African American teaching hospital. *Photograph courtesy of Bette Wheeler-Strictland, daughter of Emma Rochelle Wheeler.*

The Wheelers labored side by side for ten grueling years, trying to provide much-needed healthcare to the African American citizens of Chattanooga, while helping the community to improve their own personal and physical well-being.

Of course, Wheeler was an entrepreneur before the word even became popular in the American vocabulary. As she began to reflect on the medical environment of Chattanooga, Tennessee, she soon realized that nothing was going to change about African American healthcare unless African Americans took matters into their own hands. With money she saved during the first ten years of medical practice, Emma Wheeler purchased two lots on the corner of East 8th and Douglas Streets. There, she had a three-story building constructed to her specifications. She had enough money to pay for one-half the total cost of the building in cash.

She wanted a facility with enough room to attend to the ever-growing medical needs of the African American community. She also dreamed of having a facility that granted full admitting privileges to African American physicians. This new facility would be a teaching hospital too—one that served as a practical training school for student nurses.

On July 30, 1915, Emma Rochelle Wheeler's vision came to life. Walden Hospital, with its thirty-bed capacity, nine private rooms and one ward of twelve beds, was officially dedicated and open for business. Walden Hospital had surgical, maternity and nursery departments. It was staffed by two house doctors and three nurses, but a total of seventeen other physicians and surgeons from the Mountain City Medical Society also used the facility and admitted their patients. On the average, the new Walden Hospital served approximately twelve patients a month.

John N. Wheeler, Emma's husband, also used the facility, but the hospital was built, paid for, managed and operated by Emma Wheeler. The hospital did so well that Emma paid off the remaining note on the building within three years of opening for business.

Wheeler served as superintendent of Walden Hospital. She personally performed many surgical procedures, but she also had to maintain long office hours as hospital manager. One of her many duties, for instance, was maintaining a school for nurses. She and John Wheeler taught and trained numerous students who dreamed of becoming nurses. Emma would go on to perform this duty for more than twenty years.

In 1925, Emma Wheeler initiated the Nurse Services Club of Chattanooga. It was the only club of its type in Chattanooga and was entirely separate from the hospital's operation. Once again, Emma Wheeler proved herself ahead of her time. Her Nurse Services Club was extremely innovative; it had a prepayment plan and offered two weeks of free hospitalization, if needed. It also offered at-home assistance given by a nurse after discharge from the hospital.

Emma Wheeler was also involved in other community activities. In 1925, she joined Emma Henry, Zenobia House and Marjorie Parker in organizing the Pi Omega Chapter of Alpha Kappa Alpha sorority, Chattanooga's first AKA Chapter.

In 1928, Emma and John Wheeler erected a new building on East 9th Street in the 500 block, just across Douglas Street. This building was slotted for more office space, and there the Wheelers practiced medicine and offered office space for other doctors. Their building had the name "Wheeler" and the year 1928 inscribed across the top.

In 1940, John N. Wheeler died, leaving Emma Wheeler to continue the family medical legacy alone. He was buried in Highland Cemetery. By 1951, Emma Wheeler had been running Walden Hospital for thirty-six years—eleven of them alone. Her health began to decline, and finally in June 1953 she decided to retire from operating and managing Walden Hospital. With her retirement, Chattanooga's first and only African American owned and operated hospital ceased operation on June 30, 1953, after thirty-eight wonderful years of services. Unfortunately, although Emma expressed hope that the Nurse Services Club would continue, it was also disbanded after the hospital ceased operation.

Despite her retirement, Emma continued to practice general medicine for awhile and received her patients on the first floor of the Walden Building. On September 12, 1957, Emma Rochelle Wheeler died in Nashville's Hubbard Hospital at the great age of seventy-five. Her family brought her body back to Chattanooga, Tennessee, the city she loved, and held funeral services at the Wiley Memorial Methodist Church. Emma Rochelle Wheeler was buried in Highland Cemetery next to her husband, John N. Wheeler.

Dr. John N. Wheeler

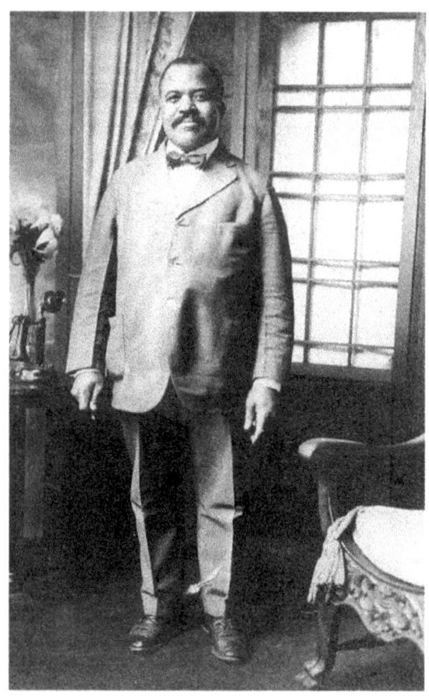

This is an early photograph of Dr. John N. Wheeler, who married Emma Rochelle in 1905. Although John would hold no interest in Walden Hospital, he would channel his patients there. *Photograph courtesy of Bette Wheeler-Strictland, daughter of Emma Rochelle Wheeler.*

Born in Kentucky in 1872, Dr. John N. Wheeler was educated in Vienna, Illinois. He was thirty-one years old when he graduated from Meharry Medical College in 1903. He graduated with a medical and surgical degree.

Immediately upon his graduation, he moved to Winchester, Tennessee, to serve the destitute African American community there. However, he returned to Nashville in 1905 to attend Emma Rochelle's graduation and to become her husband. He worked side by side with Emma for over thirty-five years.

During his time as a physician in Chattanooga, he was also treasurer of the Mountain City Medical Society and was a charter member of Emma's Nurse Services Club with its five hundred members. He was also a member of the Men's Service Club of the First Congregational Church, where he attended.

John N. Wheeler died in his rooms at Walden Hospital on April 3, 1940, after wrestling with an illness for several weeks. He was buried in Highland Cemetery.

8.

African American Hospitals in Chattanooga

Walden Hospital

First African American Hospital in Chattanooga

Walden Hospital was the first African American hospital in Chattanooga, Tennessee. It was also the first and only African American teaching hospital in Chattanooga, Tennessee. Walden was founded, built and managed by Dr. Emma Rochelle Wheeler.

Walden Hospital had a bed capacity of thirty patients—a staggering number at the time. There were nine private rooms with two beds in each room, and one large ward with twelve beds in it. There were surgical, maternity and nursery departments, and Walden had a house staff of two, with three nurses onboard, one of them a recent graduate from a nursing school. But perhaps best of all, Walden was happily patronized by seventeen physicians and surgeons, some of whom were white doctors with Negro patients. The average load was twelve patients per month.

Walden Hospital was dedicated to the community on July 30, 1915, with an afternoon and evening dedicatory service that turned into a gala community event. The afternoon "exercises" were held at the First Baptist Church, which was also located on East 8th Street. The Reverend E. Moore, pastor of the St. James Baptist Church, gave the invocation. Dr. O.W. James, owner of the East Side Pharmacy and the James Building of 9th Street fame, and co-owner of the James and Allen Drug Company, was the master of ceremonies and gave the introductory speech. Prominent members of the city made their appearance, such as Mayor Littleton, Dr. E.B. Wise, the city physician, Lee Suggs, representing a group called the NCCDBSS[64] convention, and Reverend Tate, who preached the sermon.

But the dedication of Walden Hospital was too important an event to be confined only to morning exercises. There were evening exercises too, which were held in the stately parlors of Walden Hospital. This time, Dr. W. A. Thompson was master of ceremonies and gave the introductory speech. Reverend Charles A. Bell gave the invocation, and businessmen, physicians and professional men from the community gave two-minute speeches. The list of physicians attending the grand opening was impressive. By now, Chattanooga was proud of its little oddity called Emma Rochelle

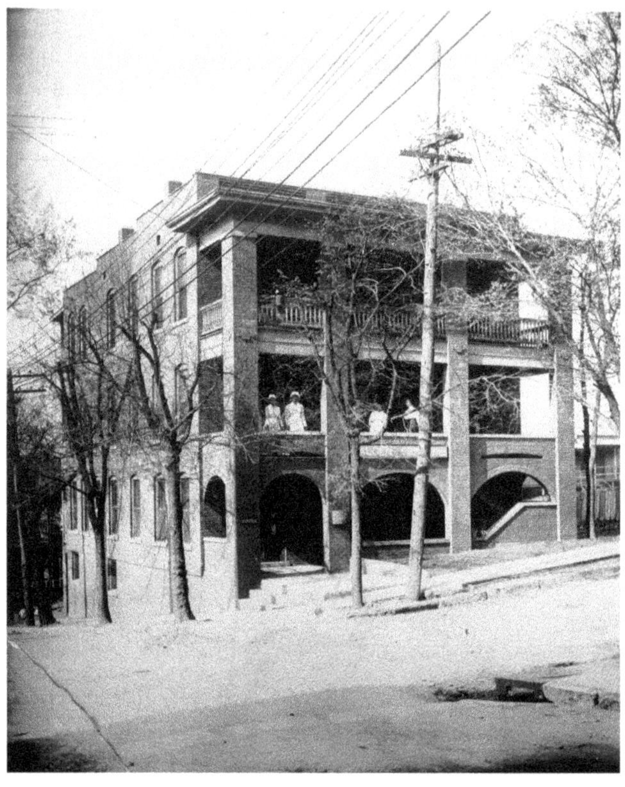

This is a 1914 photograph of Walden Hospital, which officially opened for business in July 1915. A closer view reveals Dr. Emma Wheeler and three of her nurses standing on the second floor balcony. The hospital, which had nine private, two-bed rooms and one large ward with twelve beds, was located at the corner of East 8th and Douglas Streets. Emma's husband, Dr. John N. Wheeler, used the facility for his practice, as did seventeen other physicians. In fact, two signs can be seen on the bottom floor entrance; one for Dr. Patton and one for Dr. Callier. The building still stands today, and has been restored to its former glory by entrepreneur and philanthropist W.C. Hunter, who was keenly interested in preserving its rich historic value. It is now used as apartments for college students who attend the University of Tennessee at Chattanooga. *Photograph courtesy of Chattanooga-Hamilton County Bicentennial Library.*

Wheeler; she had come to Chattanooga as its first and only female African American physician, but now the community knew her as an innovator and entrepreneur.

Drs. Looney, Moore, Stephens, Patton, Callier, Douglas, Taylor, Foster, Fields, Allen, Simms, Sharp, Valentine, Durroh, Eberhardt, Wilson, Cabinet, Frierson and Macker all came to sum up their impression of Walden Hospital, and to wish Dr. Emma Rochelle Wheeler well. Professor Howse and Mr. George Washington Franklin, undertaker and owner of the G.W. Franklin Funeral Home, represented the businessmen and professionals of the community.

A Nursing School

In 1925, ten years after its opening, Emma Wheeler had another innovative idea. She believed that Chattanooga's Negro community needed more than just a healthcare facility where they could be admitted in times of need. She believed that the African American community needed a nursing school, where aspiring African American healthcare professionals could learn how to teach other people in the community about healthcare.

In 1898, Dr. Thomas William Haigler had started a little school called the Chattanooga National Medical College, where he educated both Negroes and whites in the medical professions. Now it was Emma's turn to start a school that would allow

African Americans to rise above such typical occupations as domestic housekeeper, farmer, cook, nanny and janitor to medical occupations such as nurse or pre-medicine. She and her husband John taught and trained scores of African Americans who dreamed of becoming nurses.

Emma Wheeler also started the Nurse Services Club. This was the only club of its type in Chattanooga and was operated entirely separate from Walden Hospital. Even Erlanger Hospital, the local white hospital, did not have a club like this one. The Nurse Services Club was a type of "wellness" club, and may well have been the first of its type in the Chattanooga area. After years of serving poverty-stricken Negroes who could barely pay the fees for an emergency procedure, Emma got the idea to invent a prepayment plan that would take care of all that. She designed the plan so that if African Americans paid money into it even while they were well, they would be guaranteed two free weeks of hospitalization when the need arose, plus they would receive at-home assistance by one of Emma's nurses after they were discharged from the hospital.[65] The price was twenty-five cents per week—a fortune at that time, certainly, but well worth it in the end.[66] No other medical establishment in Chattanooga had ever offered such perks before Wheeler started her Nurse Services Club, although others would quickly follow her example.

Walden Hospital's Civil Duty

Walden Hospital did not only perform a medical duty to the community, it performed a civil duty also. When World War II became a harsh reality in 1939, Chattanooga African Americans were fully expected to serve their country like the rest of the males across the nation. The problem was that the same prejudice and discrimination prevalent in the early years still stood in 1939. Ready and able young Negro boys needed to pass their physicals before they could be inducted into the service and sent off to fight for the country that still did not, as yet, see them as equals.

Unfortunately, these boys were not allowed into the city hospitals for their physicals because the city hospitals were for whites only. But Walden Hospital solved that problem. One by one these brave young boys lined up at the fire escape stairs located on the right side of Walden Hospital and patiently waited their turn for the physical exam. Emma Wheeler prepared a sunny room with large windows on the very top floor, and there she arranged the tables and necessary equipment.[67] And as each frightened, hopeful, skittish or courageous recruit stepped over the threshold, Chattanooga's only female Negro physician performed the very examination that the white doctors would not.

In another instance, Walden Hospital fixed the social blunder associated with the Chattanooga Streetcar Company. The Chattanooga Streetcar Company employed many African Americans. They were expected to be in excellent physical condition; however, they too were turned away from area white hospitals when they went for physical exams. Walden Hospital opened its doors to these employees.

Walden Hospital most certainly served the African American community in many ways. The Nurse Training School helped African Americans to better themselves. Walden's Nurse Services Club was like healthcare insurance for people with low incomes. And Walden Hospital served the public by accepting African American patients who were not welcome in other scenarios.

In short, Walden Hospital was, for a time, everything to everyone in the African American community.

CARVER MEMORIAL HOSPITAL

When the people of Chattanooga recognized that a larger hospital program was needed for African American citizens, Chattanooga formally dedicated Carver Hospital in July 1947. At that time, Carver was believed to be the only municipally owned hospital in the United States for "colored people." It had fifty beds and was manned entirely by African American personnel. Its entire support came from Chattanooga taxpayers.

The hospital's existence was said to have resulted from the effort of Roy McDonald, publisher of the *Chattanooga Free Press* and chairman of the city's hospital board. Carver was named for the late George Washington Carver, one of the nation's foremost and most well-known scientists.

An attorney by the name of M.B. Finkelstein had purchased the former West-Ellis property and then generously made it available to the city. He went on to pledge a fully equipped operating room by the time the hospital opened its doors. The *Chattanooga Times* February 1945 article seized the opportunity to broadcast Mr. Finkelstein's generosity and made a veiled "all-call" for other citizens to take part in the historic event by donating equipment and facilities to make the hospital a success.

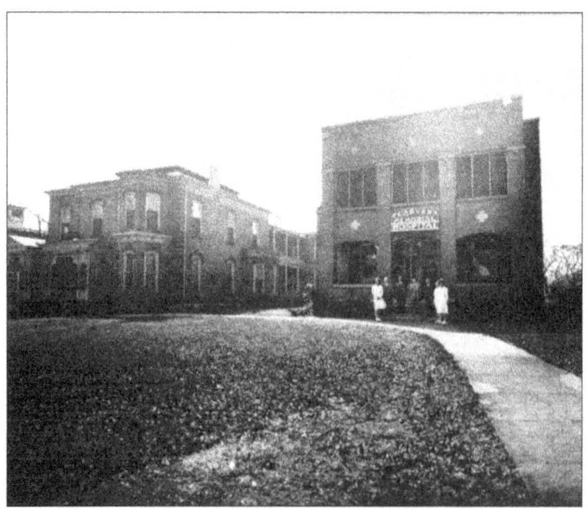

A 1950 photograph of Carver Memorial Hospital. *Courtesy of E.Y. Chapin, Walter Cline and Frank F. Stoops of the Chattanooga Half Century Club.*

In the meantime, the local newspapers sprang to life with articles about the glory of the upcoming "one of a kind" Negro hospital. It would have an auxiliary organization, nurse's aides and a group called "Gray Ladies." It would utilize the prepaid hospitalization plan (started by Emma Wheeler) that was already in place at Erlanger and T.C. Thompson Children's hospital, and which would be extended to cover the new "colored" hospital.

On February 2, 1945, the *Chattanooga Times* printed the opinions of the hospital trustees:

> *The hospital* [Carver] *will start with provisions for 50 beds. If properly managed and adequately directed this medical center for colored patients should become one of the worthwhile institutions of the community. When the colored staff have demonstrated their ability to conduct the hospital the authorities should double the capacity and add a school for the training of colored nurses. It is a great work and worthy of greatest effort. Good fortune attend the undertaking.*

By August 1945 an elevator was purchased for the new Negro hospital, and a contractor was set to install a furnace and boiler to make the steam necessary to sterilize the equipment. To insure public interest, officials at Erlanger and T.C. Thompson's hospitals met with Drs. N.B. Callier, J.G. Conyers, T.E. Taylor and L.L. Patten of the Mountain City Medical Society to plan a "sample room" that visitors could examine to see for themselves what the hospital would be like when all the remodeling and refurbishing was finished. Then they planned no fewer than two open house events that were sure to snare the interest of every single African American in the community and sway them in the direction of the new hospital.

On Sunday, June 15, 1947, Mr. Roy McDonald, chairman of Erlanger Hospital's Board of Trustees, dedicated the Carver building and presented it to the Negroes of Chattanooga. There were speeches and fanfare, and photographers milled about taking snapshots that would run in the Tuesday, June 17, 1947, *Times* newspaper. One photograph showed three African American nurses and Superintendent E.L. Crozier inspecting an incubator in the baby nursery department. Another snapshot captured the bright, smiling faces of nine African American nurses, meticulously groomed and ready for community service.

The *Times* newspaper article boasted of how Carver Memorial contained the best equipment obtainable, due partly to the $80,000 contribution made by Erlanger Hospital and the city and county.

Ever gracious, Dr. Emma R. Wheeler, founder and operator of Walden Hospital, spoke these words about Carver:

> *I am so glad that there are hospitals in Chattanooga that are always open to us, and particularly have I been thankful for Carver Memorial Hospital and what it means to Negroes, not only for medical and surgical care, but for the encouragement it gives to young Negroes to become doctors. I have tried to encourage many young men to study medicine, and many young women, too, for although few women of my day and generation become doctors, it always seemed to me to be a natural career for women.*[68]

Part IV

The Thriving African American Community of Yesterday

I have often thought that to the colored man of forty and upwards, who stops to reflect upon the changes in his condition the last twenty-five years have brought about, these changes must appear as wonderful as the tales of the Arabian Nights.

Only think of it! Twenty-five years ago a race of slaves, with no prospect of ever escaping from the house of bondage! In the eye of the law, only property like the master's mule or his ox. Liable at any time to be sold or to have his wife and children sold away from him, never again to meet them. The gates of knowledge barred against him, and the law making it a crime to teach him to read even in the Book of Life. Now a freeman, his own master, his labor his own, his wife and children his own, churches of his own, in which to worship God; schools for his children, supported for the most part by his former masters, asylums for the orphan children of his race, and he himself entitled to all the rights of an American citizen.

Are not these wonderful changes? Do not we live in a wonderful time?

Verily, these are God's doings and they are marvelous to our eyes.

—Excerpt from an address by the Honorable Xenophon Wheeler to the African American citizens of Chattanooga, Tennessee, during the dedication ceremony for the Steele Home for Needy Children, May 4, 1886.

9.

The Thriving African American Community

This chapter lists only a sampling of the thriving Chattanooga African American community of yesterday. These were some of the more visible citizens; however, this is not intended to be an exhaustive list of the "who's who" of the early years.

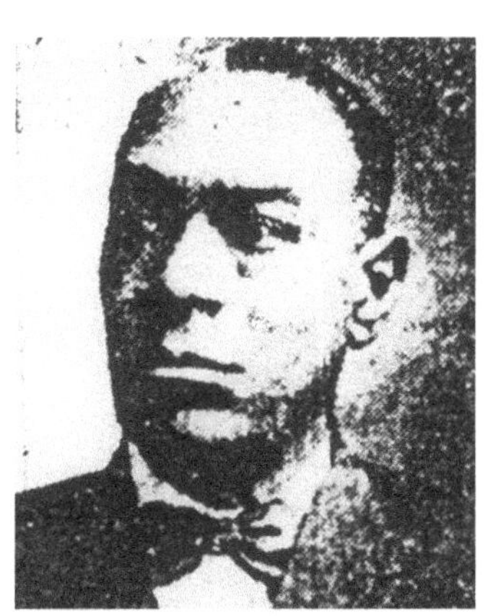

Squire Burge

Mr. J.G. Burge, also known as "Squire Burge," was an African American attorney who practiced law in Chattanooga's early years. He was admitted to the Chattanooga Bar in January 1892.

This is a photograph of J.G. Burge, attorney, who was admitted to the Chattanooga Bar in January 1892. *Photography courtesy of the* Chattanooga Times, *July 1, 1928, Jubilee No. 25.*

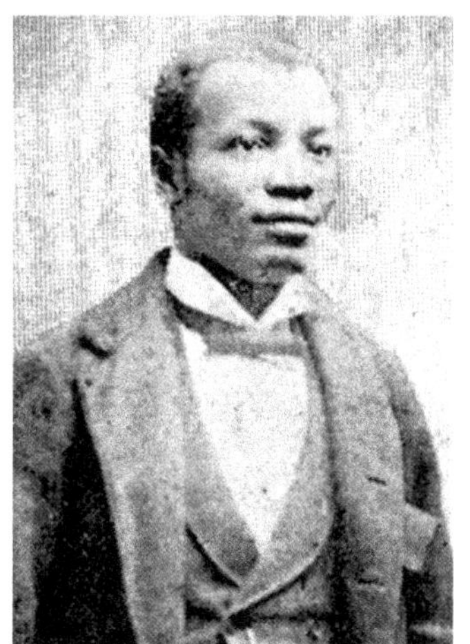

John Drain

Barber

John Drain was born in Upson, Georgia. He located in Chattanooga in 1870. He was in the barber business for over eighteen years, and owned and managed two of the most prominent and successful shops in the city. The Drain Barber Shop was both attractive and impressive, and was said to be frequented by society's best.

This is a 1904 photograph of John Drain, a barber who was credited with raising the standards of all journeymen barbers with his outstanding business practices. *Photograph courtesy of* 1904 Biography and Achievements of the Colored Citizens of Chattanooga *by J. Bliss White.*

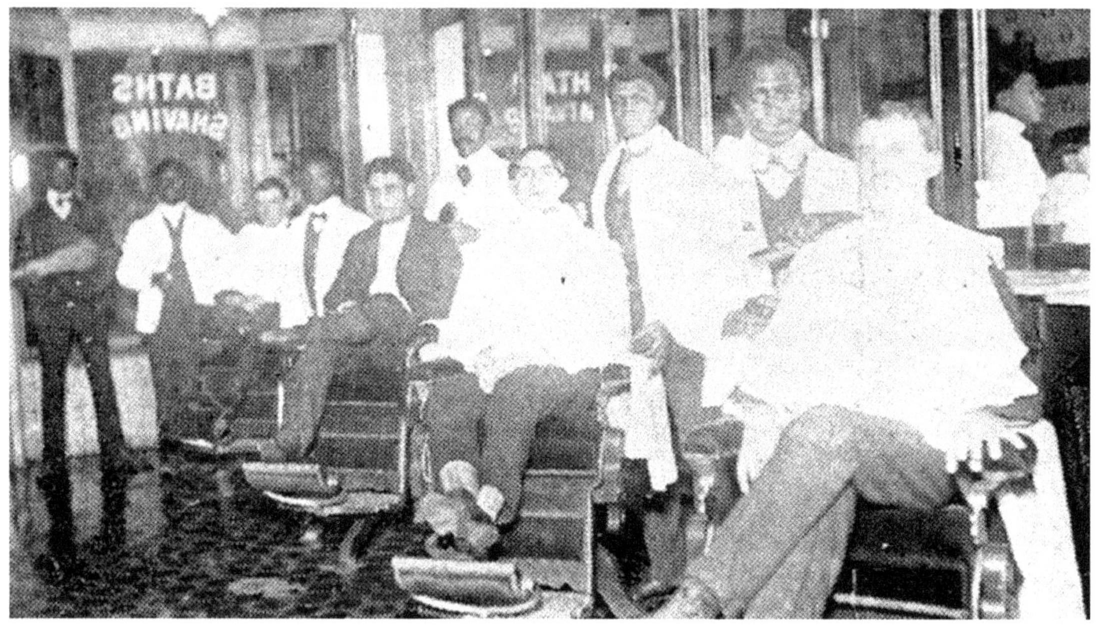

John Drain's Barber Shop was both attractive and impressive. *Photograph courtesy of* 1904 Biography and Achievements of the Colored Citizens of Chattanooga *by J. Bliss White.*

Drain was credited with establishing Chattanooga city's system of hack stands. City hacks were a sort of horse-drawn taxi service. Drain is also said to have raised the standards of all journeymen barbers with his outstanding business practices.

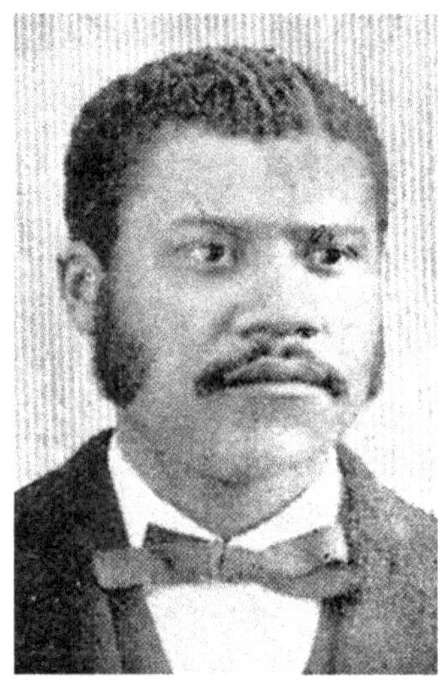

J.P. EASLEY

Attorney at Law

J.P. Easley was born in Trenton, Georgia, and attended school at Atlanta University. He came to Chattanooga in 1878, and taught school here for many years. He served as circuit court clerk for Hamilton County, Tennessee, for four years. Afterward, he was admitted to the Chattanooga Bar and had many clients from the entire community. He was eventually allowed to practice law in all courts of the United States. His office was located at 16½ East 7th Street.

J.P. Easley served as circuit court clerk for Hamilton County for four years. Afterward, he was admitted to the Chattanooga Bar and served many clients throughout the community. *Photograph courtesy of* 1904 Biography and Achievements of the Colored Citizens of Chattanooga *by J. Bliss White.*

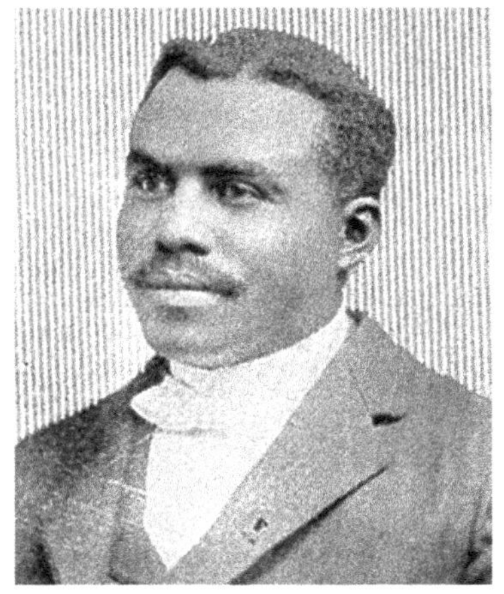

G.W. Franklin was an undertaker, but he also owned a blacksmith shop, a hack line and a wood and coal yard. *Photograph courtesy of* 1904 Biography and Achievements of the Colored Citizens of Chattanooga *by J. Bliss White.*

G.W. Franklin

Undertaker

George Washington Franklin was born in Georgia and raised in Rome, Georgia. His father taught him the blacksmith trade at the age of ten, and before long he was operating four businesses of his own: A blacksmith business, a hack line (taxi line, using horse-and-buggy), a wood and coal yard, and an undertaker's business.

Although Franklin did well at all four businesses, he decided he could only concentrate on one business at a time, so he chose to continue the undertaking business.

He relocated to Chattanooga, Tennessee, on December 7, 1894. According to the record books, he did such a superb job as undertaker that he restored the public confidence, which had been deeply shaken due to abuse by other African American undertakers. His hearses were considered equal to those of white undertakers, and he was esteemed among both races.

Mr. Franklin was also the owner of some of the finest real estate in Chattanooga, including two large cemeteries (East View and Pleasant Garden), a small truck farm on Missionary Ridge, and a 111-acre farm that contained coal, iron ore and fine timber. He even owned half the block where his mortuary was located.

Franklin credited his friend, Booker T. Washington, and the National Negro Business League with inspiring and encouraging him. He was married and had two children. He actively included his wife and children in the family business and also provided employment for seven other workers.

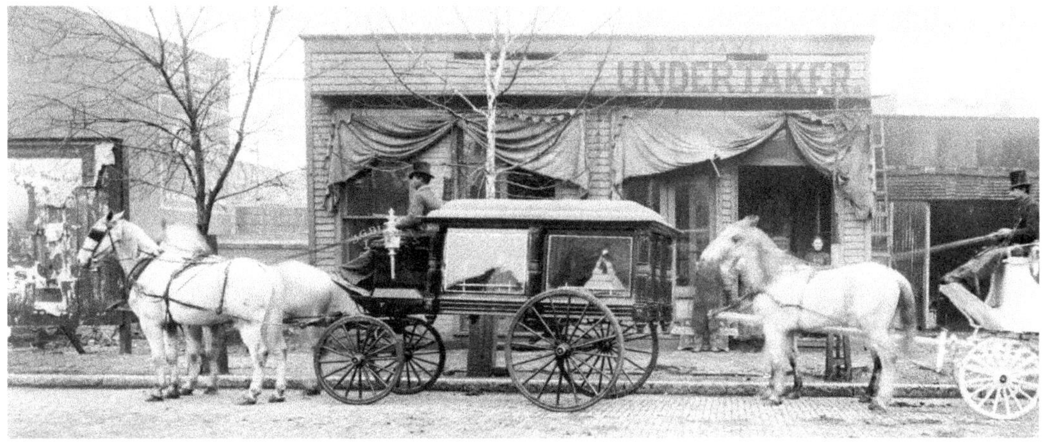

This 1899 photograph shows the G.W. Franklin Funeral Home, which was the forerunner of the Franklin-Strictland Funeral Home. *Photograph courtesy of the Library of Congress Archives, ©1899.*

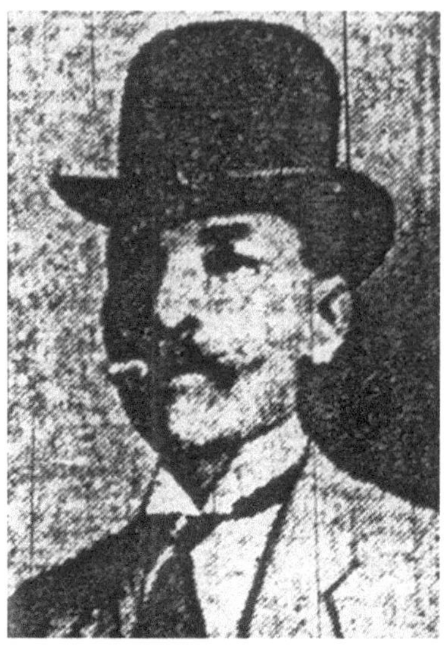

An early photograph of the prosperous John G. Higgins, who was a barber and an inventor. John owned the O.K. Shaving Parlor and eleven other tonsorial parlors. John invented the Eureka Straightening Comb, which was guaranteed to straighten the hair of "colored" people. He was the grandfather of Josephine Wheeler, the daughter-in-law of Dr. Emma Rochelle Wheeler. *Photograph courtesy of the* Chattanooga Times, *1928.*

John G. Higgins

The wealthy John G. Higgins was another successful African American barber in Chattanooga in the late 1800s and early 1900s. Higgins owned the O.K. Shaving Parlor, which was located at 911 Market Street and was considered one of the prettiest shops in the city. Higgins's shop was said to be frequented by some of Chattanooga's best citizens.

In addition to the O.K. Barber Shop, Higgins also owned eleven other prominent tonsorial shops. He was the inventor of the wildly successful Eureka Straightening Comb, which was "guaranteed to straighten the hair of colored folks." According to Higgins's granddaughter, Josephine Dorsey-Wheeler, daughter-in-law of Dr. Emma Rochelle Wheeler, Higgins committed suicide after being repeatedly pressured to sell his company.[69]

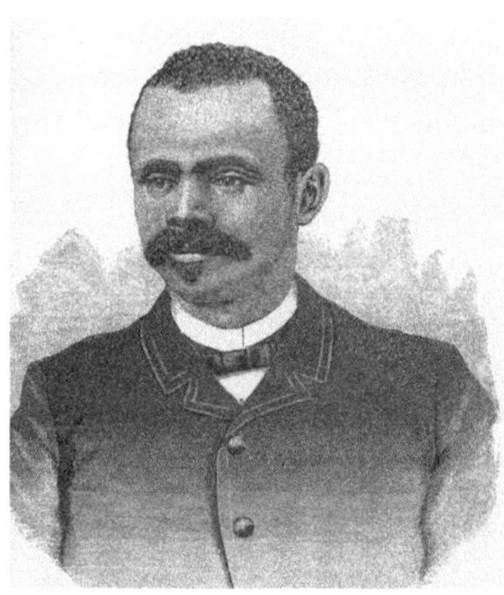

This is a photograph of John James Irvine, the first African American elected to the Hamilton County Circuit Court in 1886. *Photograph courtesy of* Men of Mark: Eminent, Progressive and Rising *by Reverend William J. Simmons and Henry McNeal Turner.*

John J. Irvine

First African American Elected to the Hamilton County Circuit Court, 1886

John James Irvine's biography is an inspiration to modern day African Americans. He overcame many odds and became a leader in Chattanooga. All text and facts were taken from *Men of Mark: Eminent, Progressive and Rising* by William J. Simmons.[70]

John James Irvine was born a slave on August 3, 1852, in Mecklenburg County, Virginia. When he was only seven years old he was ordered to work for a man who lived five miles from his birthplace. His mother tried to prepare him for the journey, but he would have to walk the entire distance without her because she had other duties on the plantation. His only companion would be a boy slightly larger than himself for whom young John was made responsible.

John cried at being separated from his mother. His new master felt sorry for him and allowed him to go home every second Sunday to see his family. Seven-year-old John would run the entire distance just to be with his mother and father.

John began a secret campaign to learn to read and often sneaked books belonging to his master. With these he was able to acquire the foundation of all his education. At fourteen years of age, or thereabout, John's mother died, and he was hired out to a farmer for $12 a year and three suits of clothing, plus all the education he could pick up on Saturday afternoons. Although he preferred to frolic his Saturdays away, he made up for this lack of learning on Sundays. At that time, he would hold the horse's reins and wait for his owner to finish worshipping in his church, and since no black person was allowed to enter the church or even look in that direction, John used this time to study his lessons.

After emancipation, John performed all types of jobs. He usually negotiated with his employers to educate him and give him room and board in exchange for manual labor, but many of them deceived him. They worked him and fed him, but rarely educated him, and usually refused to pay him the money he was due for his labor.

John reunited with his father and three of his brothers in 1868, and this family of five decided to move further south to find work. They worked for General Nathan B. Forrest, a Confederate military man notorious for his savagery toward African American Civil War soldiers in the infamous Fort Pillow Massacre. Under Forrest's supervision, the five men worked three months helping to build the Selma, Marion & Memphis Railroad.

John also tried his hand working two years as a house servant, but only received a $9 salary the first year, and $11 the second. He soon decided that such meager pay was not worth what he had to endure as a house boy, so he moved to Carthage, Alabama, to work on the Alabama & Chattanooga Railroad. He worked there for six months, but the company suddenly folded and John never received a penny in salary for his hard labor.

Next, John worked for a year on the Louisville & Nashville Railroad, eventually being selected as a fireman on the road. This position paid him $2.25 per day. While he served, John developed a keen interest in machinery. He moved to Chattanooga, Tennessee, and promptly secured employment as a stationery engineer.

In 1882 John was nominated as constable of the Fourteenth Civil District, Hamilton County. He ran again two years later and received much approval from both African Americans and whites. Both races found him to be honest and hardworking.

According to *Men of Mark*, John conceived and patented an "oil cup" during his years as a stationery engineer. Oil cups were used to lubricate trains—the major form of transportation in those days. A search of the United States Patent and Trademark Office records has revealed no such patent, but research continues.

Many of the best mechanics in the county were said to have endorsed John's oil cup as the most complete of its kind. Although John did not continue to market his invention after he won his nomination, the oil cup was said to have brought him considerable amounts of money in his day.

In 1886 at the age of thirty-four, John James Irvine was nominated without opposition to the position of Hamilton County Circuit Court clerk. He was the first African American in Chattanooga, Tennessee, to ever hold that position. He won over a popular white Democrat and a white Republican by a 1,700-vote majority.

His new position paid him approximately $3,000 a year, roughly equivalent to over $50,000 in the new millennium. His estimated wealth, which may have been due largely to the popularity of his patented oil cup, was $10,000, roughly equivalent to over $194,746.90 in the new millennium. John James Irvine was a member of the A.M.E. Church of Chattanooga, Tennessee.

A September 3, 1895, newspaper article demonstrated how John James Irvine encouraged African Americans of his day to stand and be counted. Following is the content of that article.

> *Called Meeting at the Court House Last Night: A very respectful assemblage of colored citizens met at the court house last night in response to the call of Division Commissioner John J. Irvine, to consider the representation of the colored people of this section of the state at the Atlanta Exposition. It was announced that all exhibits of colored people would be delivered free by the members of the Southern Railway and Steamship* [word indistinguishable] *until Sept. 15, except a charge of six cents per hundred for terminal expenses, and it was urged that this liberal encouragement should bring out a large and representative exhibit.*
>
> *After some discussion a resolution was adopted asking the city council and the county court to make a small appropriation, as has been done at Nashville, Memphis and Knoxville, to meet the expenses of a superintendent for this division.*
>
> *Commissioner Irvine thinks there will be a number of exhibits from this section but says that the people are really too poor to make much of a showing. However, he expects to have more encouraging returns later on.*[71]

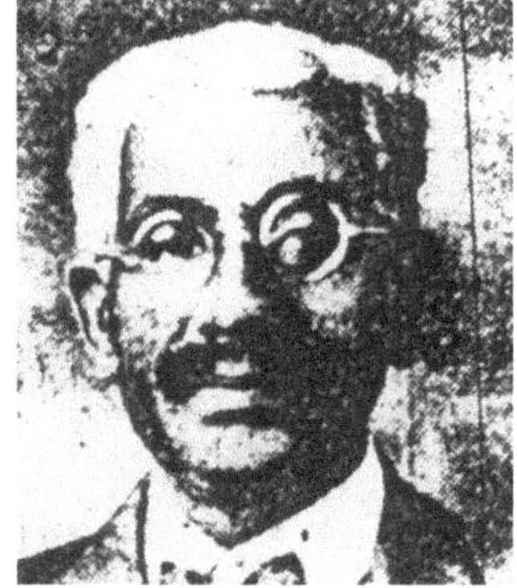

GEORGE W. JACKSON

Wood and Coal Dealer

George W. Jackson was a wood and coal dealer, and owned a prosperous business called Jackson's Wood and Coal Yard on 10th and E. Streets. As proprietor of this very necessary business, Jackson apparently built the business into an outstanding example of Negro accomplishment.

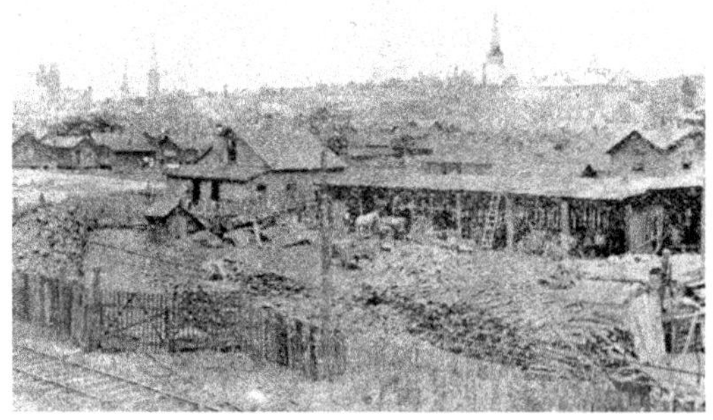

Above left: This is an early photograph of the distinguished George W. Jackson, owner of Jackson's Wood and Coal Yard. *Photograph courtesy of the* Chattanooga Daily Times, *1928, Jubilee No. 25.*

Left: Jackson's Wood and Coal Yard, located at the corner of 10th and E Streets. *Photograph courtesy of* 1904 Biography and Achievements of the Colored Citizens of Chattanooga *by J. Bliss White.*

John Lovell

Wealthy and Popular

John Lovell was a freeborn Negro, the son of a Negro woman and a wealthy white planter. Although he never acquired an education, Lovell was afforded the trades of a tinner and a barber when he was still very young and these professions helped him get his start in life.

When Lovell located to Chattanooga in 1863, he had only fifty cents in his pocket. The city of Chattanooga was almost completely covered in tents at the time Lovell arrived, and he quickly secured a tent of his own and went into the barber business. At that time, barber shops—or "tonsorial parlors," as they were sometimes called—were practically unheard of, and Lovell's new business quickly caught on. Lovell formed a partnership with George Sewell, one of the early pioneer barbers of Chattanooga. Together they made a steady income.

The barber business did not bring Lovell the fast money he was seeking, so he soon began to use the tinning skills he had learned while he was still a child. A tinner was a person who made or repaired tinware, and for a time Lovell's tinning business brought him a steady amount of money. But soon Lovell abandoned the tinning profession because he felt it moved too slowly. He then began to sell whiskey in a tent on Carter Street, and this whiskey business caught on fast. At last Lovell began to make the fast money about which he had always dreamed.

Lovell soon began to plan what he would do with his money. Uncle Bill Lewis—the veteran Chattanooga blacksmith—was another extremely wealthy African American, and he and Lovell decided to go into business together. Actually, Uncle Bill was Lovell's uncle, and the two of them began to invest in prime real estate in the Chattanooga area.

First they bought property on High Street between 4th and 5th Streets and sold it at a handsome profit. They made other investments together too, and continued to make a steady stream of money.

In the meantime, Lovell decided to buy some property that ran from Market Street to Georgia Avenue, between 9th and 10th Streets. There he decided to construct a two-story brick building and turn it into a saloon and general resort for "colored" people. He called his establishment the Mahogany Hall and offered his eager customers drinking, dancing, gambling and prostitutes. John had no trouble making large amounts of money from this establishment, but there was a down side. The saloon quickly became known as one of the most disreputable houses in the city and was raided time and again by the police.

Still, John's wealth increased and he became quite possibly the wealthiest black man in Chattanooga. He even purchased a large farm that spread across Missionary Ridge and beyond Sherman Heights. There he dealt with purebred race horses, and this sport brought him in contact with some of Chattanooga's most prominent citizens.

John's wealth was the stuff of legends. It was once rumored that he was worth over $150,000. It was also rumored that he even declined a $55,000 offer that some anonymous bidder made on his Market Street property!

But despite the rumors, John's life was not without its challenges. In fact, he made and lost several fortunes in his lifetime. He lost his first fortune acting as security for other persons and making bad investments. He then drove a water cart and made another fortune.

Although John's obituary does not go into detail about his water business, it has been documented that many an innovative man earned his fortune carting fresh spring water to various neighborhoods...and this during a time when freshwater was almost nonexistent.

George W. Sewell

Veteran Barber

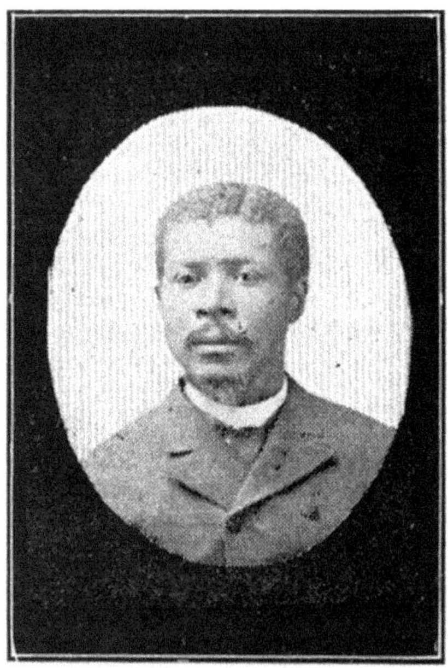

George Sewell, pioneer barber. *Photograph courtesy of* 1904 Biography and Achievements of the Colored Citizens of Chattanooga *by J. Bliss White.*

George W. Sewell was born in Shelby County, Tennessee, on September 20, 1842, and settled in Chattanooga, Tennessee, in 1863. He was a barber by trade, and by 1904 he had been in the barber business longer than any other African American in the area.

Sewell was a very public-spirited man and was considered a pioneer of Chattanooga. He was at one time a member of the county court and the board of mayors and aldermen. He was the federal court crier for twenty years, and was the father of eight successful children. One of his sons was Dr. Charles Sewell, well-known at that time and residing in Washington, D.C.

Sewell was a hardy man, evident by the fact that he had survived the deadly yellow fever epidemic of 1878, which had taken many lives in Chattanooga.

One note of historical interest involves George Sewell's attempt to forestall the hanging of Henry Lawson, a Negro accused of raping a white woman in 1881. Sewell and two other prominent Negroes of the time listened to Lawson's claim that he "committed the deed, but with the woman's consent." Sewell then wrote a hasty letter to then governor Alvin Hawkins in Nashville, Tennessee, dated September 2, 1881, in an attempt to save Lawson's life. Unfortunately, Governor Hawkins denied the plea, and Lawson was hanged on September 2, 1881.

J.A. Strictland

Merchant; President, Rising Sun Manufacturing Company

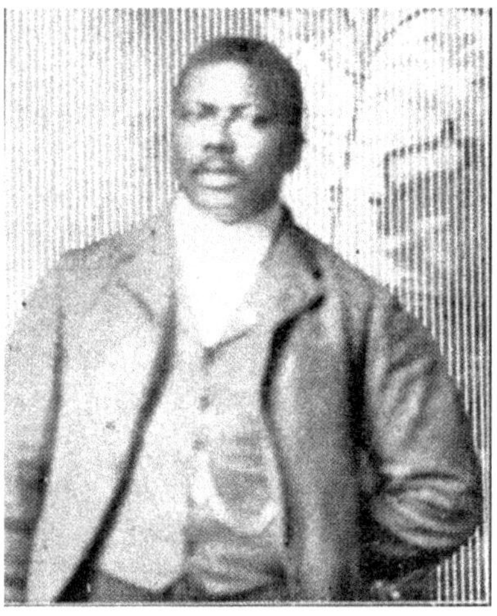

J.A. Strictland, merchant and president of the Rising Sun Manufacturing Company. *Photograph courtesy of* 1904 Biography and Achievements of the Colored Citizens of Chattanooga *by J. Bliss White.*

J.A. Strictland was born in Lawrenceville, Georgia, on April 4, 1864. He came to Chattanooga, Tennessee, in 1866. He learned the moulder's trade on a farm, but later used his savings to go into business for himself.

It is not known what type of business he had, but it is known that the business was not successful, so he later opened a grocery and general merchandise store at 826 Frank Street (14th Street). He became one of the most successful merchants among African Americans in Chattanooga.

Strictland promoted and served as president of the Rising Sun Manufacturing Company and worked toward making it a grand enterprise. He was married, had one son and lived at 217 Grove Street.

The Rising Sun Manufacturing Company was managed and operated entirely by African Americans. They specialized in stoves, grate baskets, fenders and fronts, stove repair and holloware. The foundry was located at 1312 Harrison Avenue.

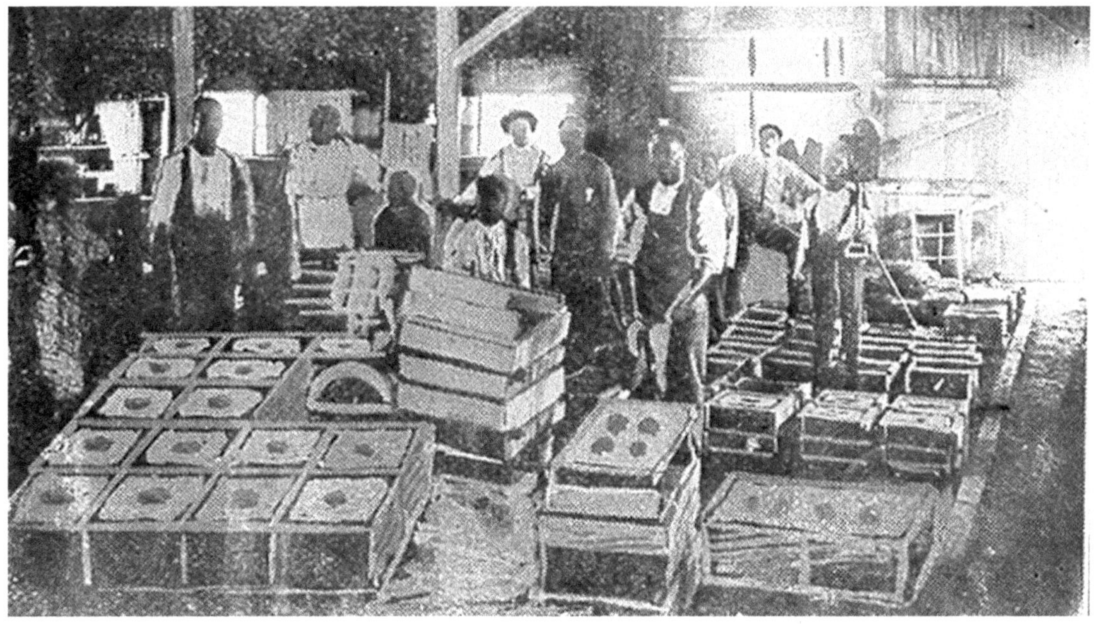

The Rising Sun Manufacturing Company was managed and operated entirely by African Americans. The company specialized in stoves, grate baskets, fenders and fronts, stove repair and holloware. The foundry was located at 1312 Harrison Avenue. *Photograph courtesy of* 1904 Biography and Achievements of the Colored Citizens of Chattanooga *by J. Bliss White.*

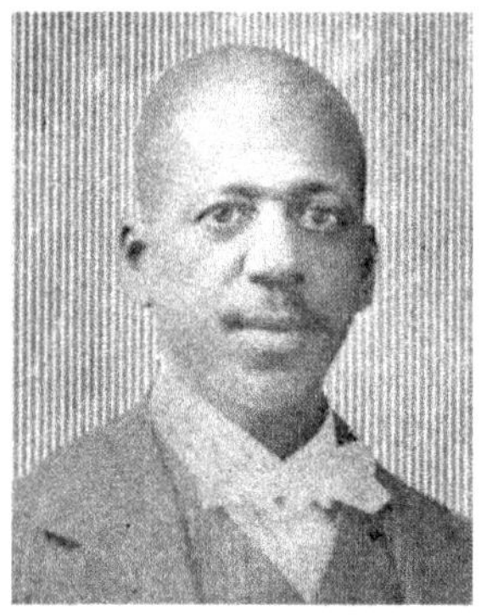

John Shepard

Manager, Chattanooga Colored Baseball Club

John Shepard was born in Marietta, Georgia. He lived for many years in Key West, Florida, and was employed on a large ocean steamer that traveled between Key West and the West Indies.

He settled in Chattanooga in 1890, and went into business for himself. Unfortunately, his business was not recorded and is therefore unknown at press time. However, it is known that Shepard was manager of the Chattanooga Colored Baseball Club. The club had the reputation of being one of the best ball clubs in the South.

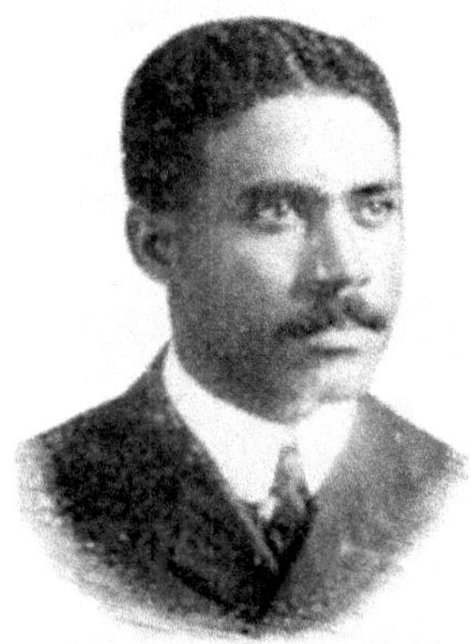

J. Bliss White

Author of Chattanooga's First African American History Book

J. Bliss White was a prominent Negro citizen in Chattanooga in the early 1900s. He was the author who boldly penned Chattanooga's Negro history, *Biography and Achievements of the Colored Citizens of Chattanooga*, in 1904. He was also a librarian, an orator and a lawyer, often practicing with his attorney father, the prominent J.W. White.

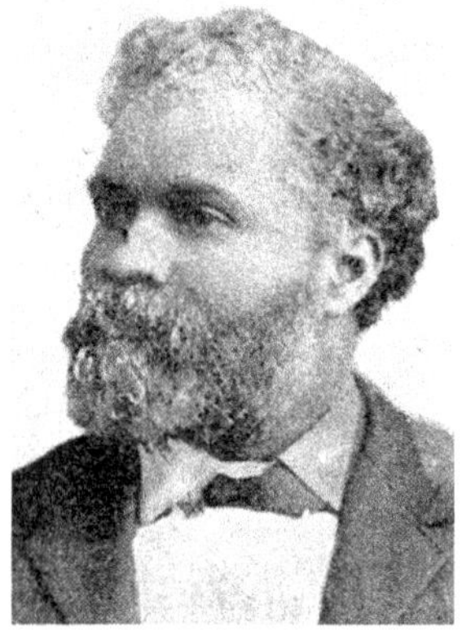

J.W. White

J.W. White was an upstanding Negro citizen who had his own illustrious career. He was a lawyer, a teacher, a justice of the peace, an alderman, a tax assessor and a poor commissioner. He had even headed Chattanooga's short-lived PennySavings Bank, a bank founded for and run by the Negroes of the community.

Top: This is an early photograph of John Shepard, who was manager of the Chattanooga Colored Baseball Club—one of the best ball clubs of the South. *Photograph courtesy of* 1904 Biography and Achievements of the Colored Citizens of Chattanooga *by J. Bliss White.*

Middle: This is a 1904 photograph of J. Bliss White, lawyer, librarian, author and orator. White was the author of the book *1904 Biography and Achievements of the Colored Citizens of Chattanooga*, from which much of the material for this book was taken. *Photograph courtesy of* 1904 Biography and Achievements of the Colored Citizens of Chattanooga *by J. Bliss White.*

Bottom: A 1904 photograph of J.W. White, father of J. Bliss White, and a teacher, justice of the peace, alderman, tax assessor, poor commissioner and lawyer. He was also the head of the PennySavings Bank of Chattanooga until its failure during the panic of 1902–3. *Photograph courtesy of* 1904 Biography and Achievements of the Colored Citizens of Chattanooga *by J. Bliss White.*

William M. Wilson

Deputy Sherriff, Postal Worker; Instrumental in Forming the Colored YMCA

William M. Wilson was born in Maryville, Tennessee, on September 25, 1868, and attended Maryville College. The date that Wilson settled in Chattanooga, Tennessee, is not known, but once a citizen of the city he was appointed deputy sheriff of the county and served in this capacity for two years. He also served as a shipping clerk in the lumber business of Duncan Pyott, and held this position until he was appointed to the position of clerk in the post office.

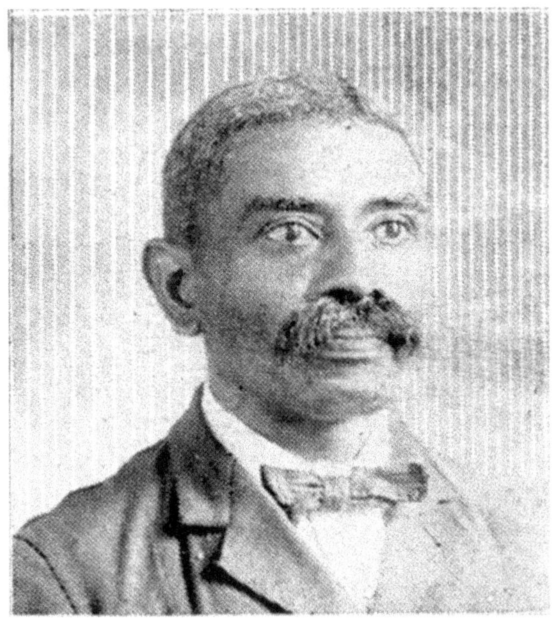

William M. Wilson, deputy sheriff of the county, postal worker, and the man responsible for the formation of the "Colored" YMCA. *Photograph courtesy of* 1904 Biography and Achievements of the Colored Citizens of Chattanooga *by J. Bliss White.*

Wilson is credited with conceiving a novel idea in recreation for African Americans in 1903. At that time, there was no "colored" branch of the YMCA. Wilson's idea was to open a public reading room for African American young men of Chattanooga, and also to provide them with a pleasant place to spend their idle time. According to early records, African Americans did not support the idea at first, but Wilson did find encouragement from other prominent individuals in the city. He also reportedly sacrificed much of his own time and money in bringing the idea to fruition.

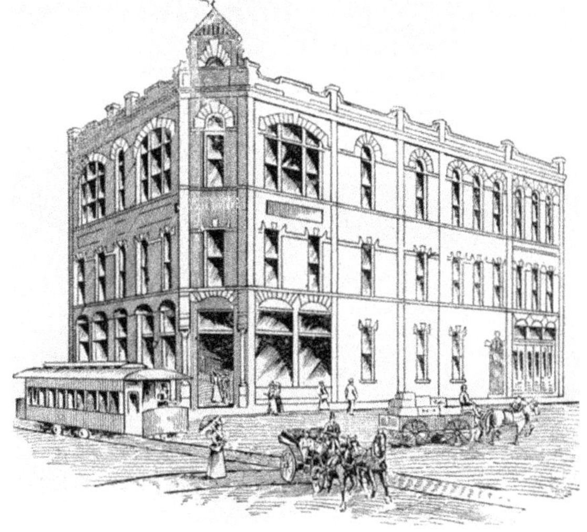

This is the "Colored" YMCA building, which was located on the corner of Georgia Avenue and East 9th Street. The building still stands today. *Image courtesy of* 1904 Biography and Achievements of the Colored Citizens of Chattanooga *by J. Bliss White.*

Wilson solicited his white friends and received more than 150 volumes of good books and papers for his proposed reading room. Once the idea caught on, both African Americans and white citizens supported the idea. The project was soon too much for one man, and steps had to be taken to aid Wilson in establishing the "colored" department of the YMCA.

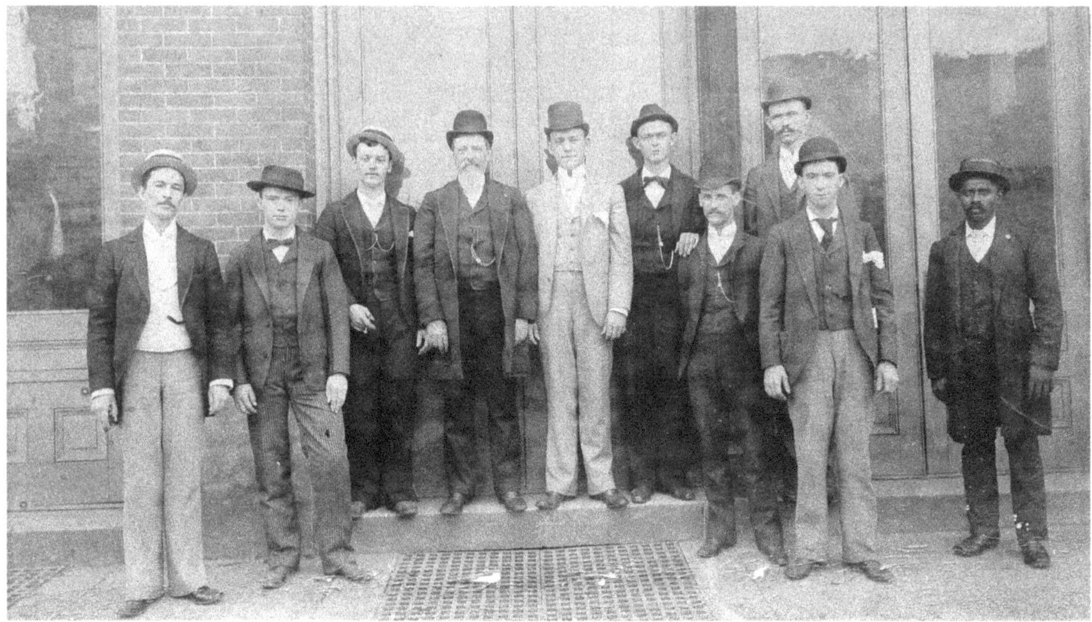

This is an 1891 photograph of William M. Wilson standing with several Carter Street postal employees. Wilson is standing on the extreme right. *Photograph courtesy of the Paul A. Heiner Collection, ©1891.*

The YMCA building for "coloreds" was located on the corner of Georgia Avenue and East 9th Street. Wilson would go on to become a member of the board of directors and vice-president of the colored YMCA. He also served as a postal carrier, servicing the Carter Street South RY Express Building. He held this position for over fourteen years.

10.

Noteworthy African American Establishments

East Side Pharmacy

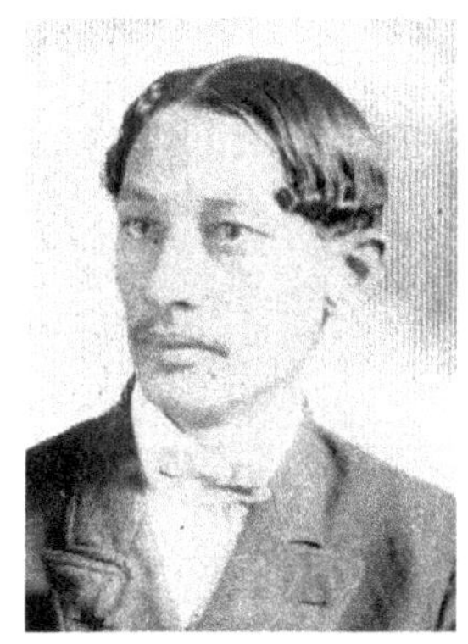

The East Side Pharmacy was at one time considered the finest Negro drugstore in the entire United States, and Negro physicians and their patients frequented the establishment.

East Side Pharmacy's prescriptions were filled by young pharmacist R. Emerson Andrews, who was a scholar graduate of Shaw University pharmaceutical department. As the legend went, Andrews spoke Latin and Greek, excelled in mathematics, and was so intellectually gifted, he graduated from Shaw's Pharmaceutical Department before the age of eighteen.[72]

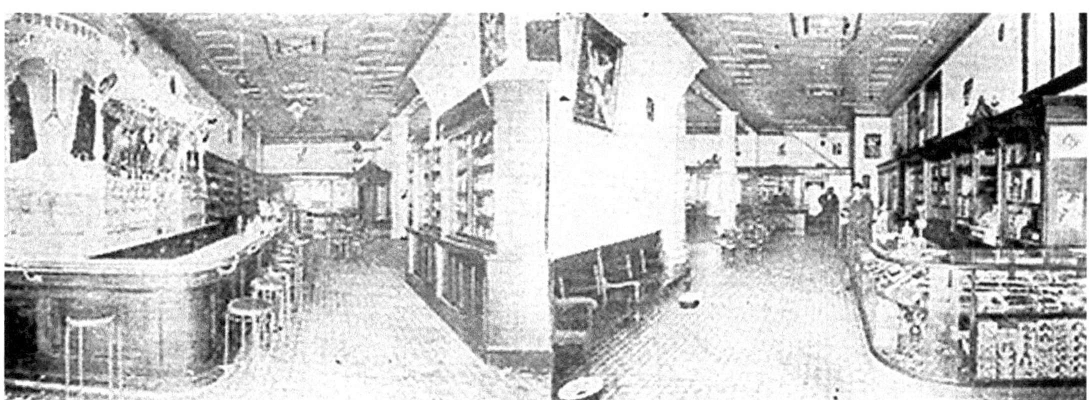

Above: The interior of the East Side Pharmacy, where R. Emerson Andrews worked. The pharmacy was located on East 9th Street inside the James Building, and was considered the finest Negro drugstore in the United States. *Photograph courtesy of* 1904 Biography and Achievements of the Colored Citizens of Chattanooga *by J. Bliss White.*

Above left: This is an early photograph of R. Emerson Andrews, who graduated from Shaw University and accepted a position as a prescription pharmacist with the James and Allen Drug Company. *Photograph courtesy of* 1904 Biography and Achievements of the Colored Citizens of Chattanooga *by J. Bliss White.*

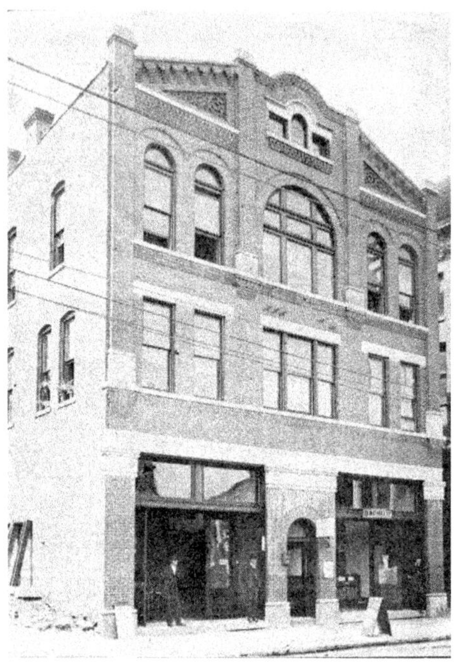

This is the James Building, owned by Dr. O.W. James. It was located on East 9th Street, and was considered one of the most modern buildings of its time. It was also the home of the famous East Side Pharmacy. *Photograph courtesy of* 1904 Biography and Achievements of the Colored Citizens of Chattanooga *by J. Bliss White.*

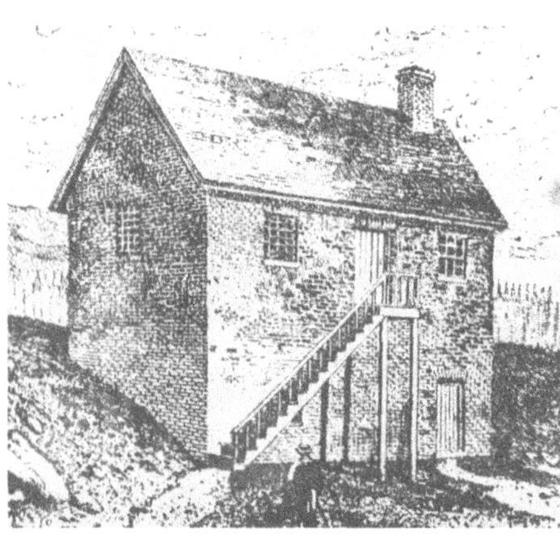

An 1863 drawing of the Swaim's Jail. *Courtesy of the Paul A. Heiner Collection, digitized by the Chattanooga-Hamilton County Bicentennial Library.*

The James Building

The James Building was a magnificent structure that was formerly located on East 9th Street. The building was owned by Dr. O.W. James and was considered "one of the most modern of its time." It had ample office space and rooms for lodging, with all the necessary sanitary arrangements. It was built entirely by African American labor, and was the home of the East Side Pharmacy.

Loomis and Hart Manufacturing

See page 29 for photograph.

The Loomis and Hart Manufacturing Company was once located at 719 East 9th Street and manufactured lumber and building materials. The company employed a large number of African American men.

As a footnote, African American men at the Loomis and Hart Manufacturing Company were known to generously donate a portion of their salary (usually twenty-five cents) toward the upkeep and feeding of the Steele Orphanage's needy children.[73] This was a large amount of money in the late 1800s and early 1900s.

Swaim's Jail

Swaim's Jail was a jail for African American criminals and runaway slaves. It was located at Lookout and 5th Streets, which is now a part of Provident Insurance Company's parking lot.

Aside from housing runaway slaves, the jail was once used to house Andrew's Raiders. Andrew's Raiders were a group of Union spies who stole a Western and Atlantic train with the intention of burning bridges to help win the Civil War.

Also known as "the Hole," Swaim's Jail was a little brick building surrounded by a high board fence. The ground sloped steeply upward so that the back of the jail was built into the hill and the front was level with the ground. The building itself was two stories high with two rooms on each floor. John Swaim, the jailor, and his family lived in the upper and lower rooms at the north end, while the rooms at the south end were used to hold the prisoners.

At the time of Andrew's Raiders' imprisonment, the prison room had no furniture and was lighted only by the candle carried by the jailer. Actually, the bottom portion was no more than a dungeon. Using a large key in the hole in the floor, the jailor would raise a heavy trapdoor and the prisoners would have to descend thirteen feet to a dungeon occupied by the "poor wretches" below. The ladder was then drawn up and the trapdoor shut.

The Hole was so dark, prisoners could see absolutely nothing. They could, however, hear and feel men moving and breathing. The only "furnishings" were buckets used for water and slop jars. The room was only thirteen feet square and was full of rats and other vermin.

There is now a historical marker commemorating the location of the Swaim's Jail. The marker is located on the rear parking lot of the old Provident Building.

Part V

Other African American Facts

Manifold are the reasons which have impelled the launching of this volume on a sea already swollen to flood tide, with contributions as innumerable as they are irrepressible, concerning the Negro today, the issue paramount, and the one which casts the heaviest shadow into the future of the American body politic. Light withers only the weak; who in the inexorable stress and strife of this world, must soonest succumb. For weakness is the crime which nature most abhors. Therefore, we cannot believe that endurance, the very essence of strength, such as the Negro has demonstrated through ages of adversity, was ever given a people destined without fruition, to perish from the earth.

—*Excerpt from* 1904 Biography and Achievements of the Colored Citizens of Chattanooga, *by J. Bliss White.*

11.

Early Tennessee State Representatives

Styles Linton Hutchins

See page 63.

Much has already been told about Styles Linton Hutchins, the Chattanooga attorney. However, aside from opening his law practice in Chattanooga in 1881 and serving as editor of the *Independent Age*, a popular black newspaper in Chattanooga, Hutchins also ran for legislature.

Hutchins was already a valiant and outstanding spokesman for civil rights, so when he decided to run for state legislature in 1886, he triumphed over his white opponent by eight votes. Hutchins was a member of the Tennessee House of Representatives' 45th Assembly from 1887 through 1888.

Hutchins served on the Education and New Counties Committee of the legislature, and succeeded in passing laws to repeal poll taxes in Chattanooga. He also helped pass laws to prevent criminals convicted in other states from testifying in Tennessee courts. He also introduced a bill to limit the use of convict labor, but that bill was not successful.

After Hutchins completed his legislative term, he returned to his Chattanooga law practice. He also held a patronage position in the revenue department of the U.S. Treasury.

Like his friend and business associate Noah Walter Parden, Hutchins was also known throughout Tennessee and Georgia as a fiery preacher who used many of his sermons to denounce racism in the South.

Styles Hutchins, Monroe Gooden and Samuel McElwee were the last African Americans to serve in the general assembly until Representative A.W. Willis Jr. was elected in Shelby County in 1964.

William C. Hodge

William C. Hodge was a man who held many jobs in Chattanooga. He held positions that included railroad agent and jailer, and continued to do so until he was elected

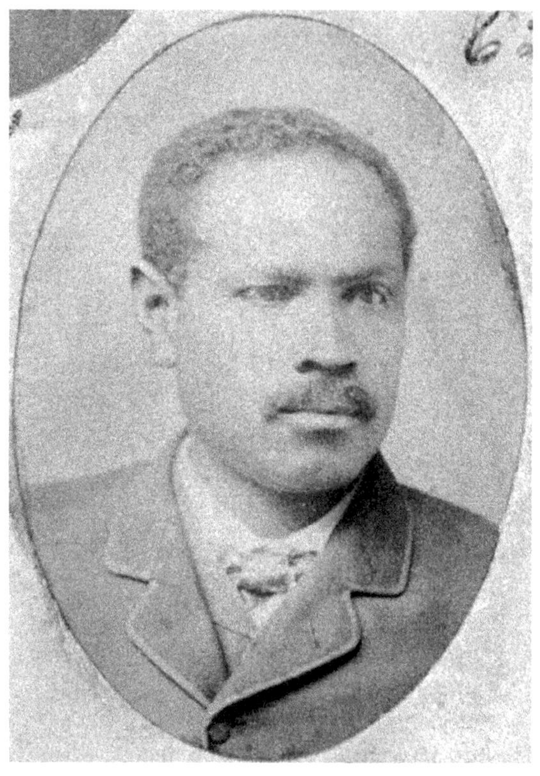

This is a photograph of William C. Hodge of Chattanooga. Hodge was a member of the 44th General Assembly, 1885–1886. *Photograph courtesy of Tennessee State Library and Archives, TSLA Collection.*

to represent Hamilton County in the 44th Tennessee General Assembly, 1885–1886. Following his legislative term, he served as a member of the Chattanooga City Council for many years.

Born in North Carolina, Hodge later settled in Chattanooga and held a number of jobs before he became a legislator: He was a contractor, a stonecutter, a house mover, a night mail transfer agent at the railroad depot, an alderman for the 4th Ward of Chattanooga and a city jailer.

During his legislative term, Hodge introduced bills to safeguard employment and voting rights for all Tennesseans. He also worked hard to overturn Chapter 130 of the Acts of 1875, which permitted discrimination on public transportation and in hotels and places of public amusement. Unfortunately, all the bills he introduced were tabled or rejected.

Hodge was a legislative candidate in 1884, the same year Tennessee's Republicans had declared themselves opposed to black candidates. He vowed it was time for white voters to get "educated up" and allow blacks to hold responsible positions. Black leaders reminded Chattanooga Republican office holders that black voters outnumbered whites 1,400 to four hundred, and that the African American voters were keeping them in office. They gently but firmly suggested that a little reciprocity would go a long way.

Hodge subsequently became the county's first black representative.

12.

Early Chattanooga African American Newspapers

All information was taken from *Standard History of Chattanooga, Tennessee* by Charles D. McGuffey.[74] Unfortunately, none of these early newspapers have survived.

The Enterprise was the first African American newspaper recorded in Chattanooga, Tennessee. It was established in the summer of 1881 by the Reverend G.W. Hays, pastor of a Methodist church. It had no press outfit (equipment or resources), and lasted only one year.

The Agitator was established in 1882 by H.C. Smith. It was a Democratic newspaper and lasted two to three months.

Justice newspaper was also established in 1882 and was owned by Horn & Wilson (Edward Horn and H.M. Wilson), both of whom were experienced politicians. After a few months, the paper's name changed to ***The Observer***, and Professor W.F. Jackson took charge of it. In all, the paper lasted only eighteen months because it too had minimal press equipment.

The Tribune was controlled by C.S. Wallace, and lasted seven to eight months.

The Age was born in the latter part of 1883 and was the brainchild of Attorneys Styles Linton Hutchins and John E. Patton. Styles Linton Hutchins would go on to become part of a team of lawyers who handled the appeal of Ed Johnson's rape conviction before he was lynched on the Walnut Street Bridge. (See page 63 for a photograph and biography of Styles Linton Hutchins, and page 60 for a biography of Ed Johnson.) This newspaper, independent in politics, lasted three to four months.

The Herald newspaper came and went in 1885. It was the brainchild of Attorney Noah Walter Parden, the second half of the legal team who handled the appeal of Ed Johnson's rape conviction in 1906. (See page 67 for a photograph and biography of Noah Walter Parden.) This paper only had a portion of the press equipment needed to survive, and it soon faded away.

The Dispatch belonged to African American barber H.A. Brown. The paper had very little equipment, and lasted two to three months.

The Liberator was a paper that came into existence under the combined efforts of W.H. Hasty and J.P. Easley in the latter part of 1886. J.P. Easley was an African American lawyer in Chattanooga. (See page 106 for a photograph and brief biography of Easley.) This paper lasted three to four months.

The Journal was a Republican newspaper that came into existence in 1896. However, it retired after only two months.

The Freeman was a Republican paper owned and operated by William Walker, an Alabama barber. The paper had no press equipment and died away quickly.

The Times-Herald was the brainchild of J.T. Pettis, a barber in Chattanooga. It was another Republican paper; however, it had no press equipment and faded away after three months.

The Southern Herald was created by Rev. T.S. Smith. With no equipment, it lasted only four to five months.

The Blade was the creation of Randolph Miller in 1898. (See page 64 for a biography of Randolph Miller.) The paper lasted until 1914 (sixteen years), and was quoted by newspapers all across the United States.

Up-To-Date was published by J.N. Daniels, date unknown.

The Search Light was created by Rev. A. Vanoy, who came to Chattanooga from Rockwood.

The Messenger was controlled by Rev. Parker of the Colored Baptist Church.

The Church Relief, which was edited by Rev. H.H. Williams, was "devoted to the normal and religious interests of the colored people" in Chattanooga. Its date of existence is unknown.

13.

Lynchings and Hangings in Chattanooga

This section lists lynchings and hangings that occurred in Chattanooga, Tennessee, after the Civil War. Other lynchings and hangings may have occurred before the Civil War; however, the Hamilton County Courthouse was struck by lightning on May 7, 1910, and the records were lost in the resulting fire. This is not an exhaustive list.

Name	Crime	Action Taken	Date
Shade Westmoreland	Murder	Hanged	1872
Henry Lawson	Rape	Hanged	September 2, 1881
Charles Williams	Murder	Lynched	September 7, 1885
Alfred Blount	Rape	Lynched	February 14, 1893
Charles Brown	Rape	Lynched	February 25, 1897
Ed Johnson	Rape	Lynched	March 19, 1906

14.

Early Record Setters

Doubtless, many records have been set by Chattanooga African Americans. However, for the purpose of this volume, only the very early achievements are included. Of these, many achievements worthy of mention may be omitted, not because it was deemed that they were not important enough to be listed, but simply because there is no access to the information or the fact was unknown. In other words, this is not an exhaustive list.

Professor James A. Henry

See page 41.

First African American principal in Chattanooga City Schools.

Bell Washington

See page 39.

First African American high school graduate, Howard High School.

Augustus Wickliff

See page 40.

First African American male high school graduate, Howard High School.

Hinton D. Alexander

See page 57–58.

First African American to go to college in Chattanooga.

DR. EMMA R. WHEELER

See page 94.

First and only African American in Chattanooga to build, own and operate an African American hospital.
First and only African American in Chattanooga to start and maintain a teaching hospital.
First woman of any race in Chattanooga to start a Nurse Services Club.
First and only African American in Chattanooga to have a project named for her.

LULA KENNEDY

First African American music teacher in Chattanooga.

JAMES CHANDLER

First African American in Chattanooga to own an automobile.
First African American to have electricity in his home.

PAUL GHOLSTON

Chattanooga's first African American city bus driver.

WILLIAM "UNCLE BILL" LEWIS

See page 54.

First African American blacksmith to locate to Chattanooga.
Put the shackles on the Andrew's Raiders.

JOHN JAMES IRVINE

See page 108.

First African American elected to the Hamilton County Circuit Court.

STYLES LINTON HUTCHINS

See page 63.

First African American admitted to the Georgia Bar.

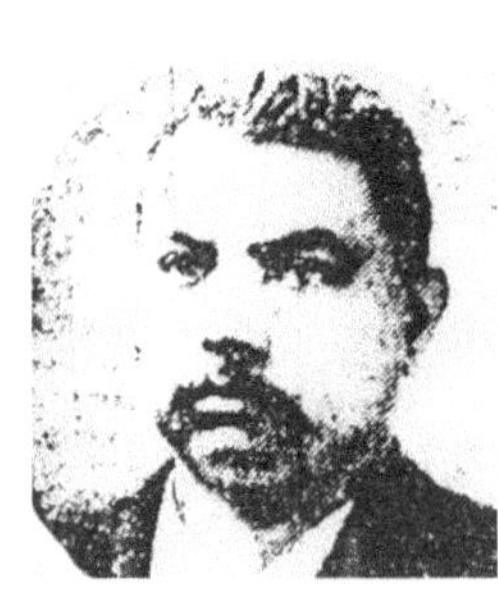

JACK HEGGIE

First African American to serve on a jury in Hamilton County, Tennessee.

This is a photograph of Mr. Jack Heggie (also listed as Jack Reggie), who was a barber and businessman. Mr. Heggie was recorded as "The First Person of his Race to Serve on a Jury in Hamilton County." *Photograph courtesy of the* Chattanooga Times, *July 1, 1928, Jubilee No. 25.*

Capt. Morris B. Glenn

See page 75, 77.

First African American to rise to position of captain of police in a major Southern city.

Kate Brown

First African American librarian of Howard High School.

Dr. O.L. Davis

See page 89.

First and only (1904) African American female dentist to graduate in the South.
First female African American to enter the practice of dentistry.

Attorney Noah Parden

See page 67.

First African American to win a stay of execution from Supreme Court.
First African American assigned the position of lead attorney in a Supreme Court case.

15.

Early Chattanooga Celebrities

Maude Browne

Not much is known about the early life of Maude Browne, the famous mezzo-soprano of the early twentieth century. It is known that Browne was born in Chattanooga, Tennessee, and graduated from Howard High School. The dates of these milestones, however, are unknown.

At the time that J. Bliss White was compiling his history of the "colored citizens of Chattanooga," Browne had already completed three successful seasons of travel with the Mason & Downs Orpheus Jubilee Singers. She and the Jubilee Singers toured the entire North and Midwest, and performed at Chautauqua in Boulder, Colorado.

Browne was said to "have a mezzo-soprano voice that was rich, rare and full of sweetness of quality...Few voices are found on the American stage that have such beautiful quality and tone production of Miss Browne's."[75]

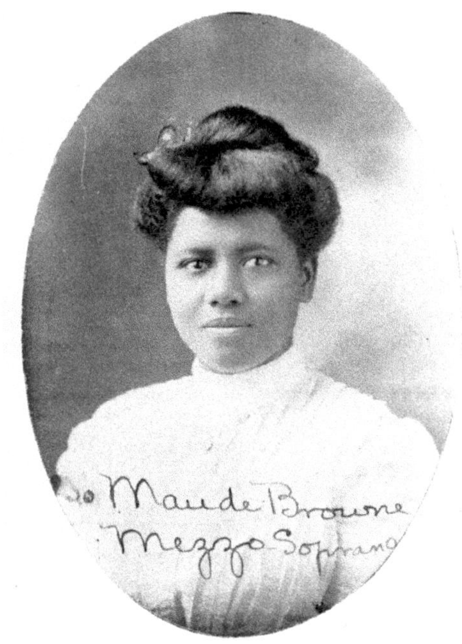

Maude Browne was a mezzo-soprano who toured the Midwest and Northern states with the Mason & Downs Orpheus Jubilee Singers. She was highly praised by music critics for having a rare voice full of rich, haunting sweetness. *Photograph courtesy of* 1904 Biography and Achievements of the Colored Citizens of Chattanooga *by J. Bliss White.*

Roland Hayes

See page 59.

Bessie Smith

See page 69.

Mary (Grandma) Walker

See page 70.

Hinton D. Alexander

See page 57.

16.

African American Markers in Chattanooga

All of the following photographs of African American markers in Chattanooga are provided courtesy of Rita Lorraine Hubbard. This is not an exhaustive list.

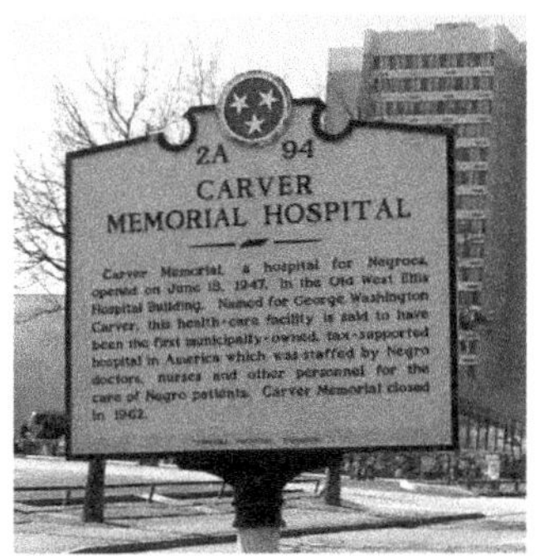

Carver Memorial Hospital
600 West M.L. King Blvd.
Chattanooga, TN 37402

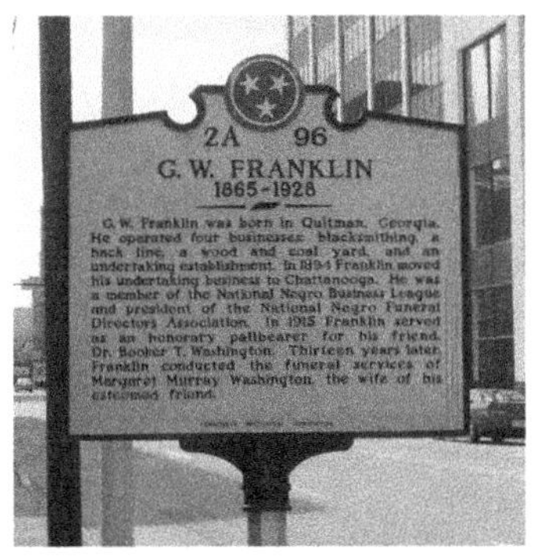

G.W. Franklin Marker
612 Chestnut Street
Chattanooga, TN 37402

The Martin Hotel Marker—See page 78.
200 E. M.L. King Blvd.
Chattanooga, TN 37403

The Mary Walker Museum Marker
3031 Wilcox Blvd.
Chattanooga, TN 37411

Sallie Crenshaw/Bethlehem Center Marker
200 W. 38th Street
Chattanooga, TN 37408

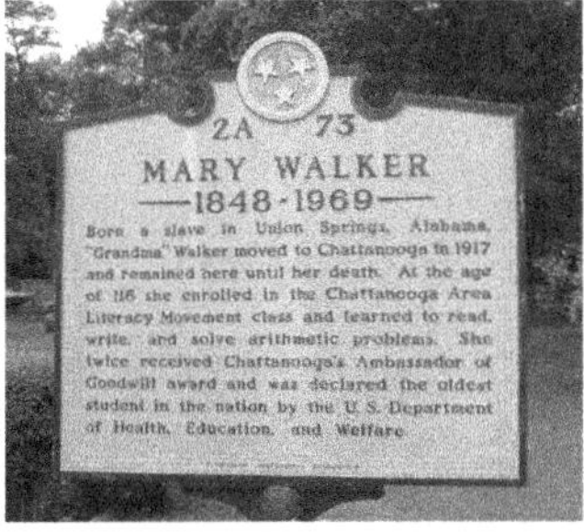

Steele Home For Needy Children Marker—See page 29.
Palmetto and 3rd-5th Streets
Chattanooga, TN 37403

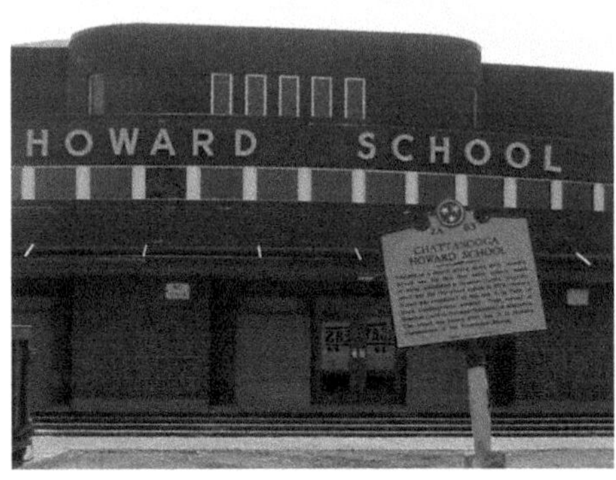

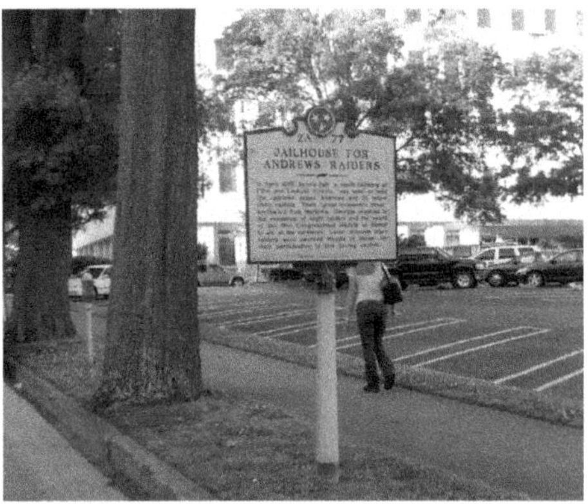

Howard High School Marker
2500 S. Market Street
Chattanooga, TN 37408

William "Uncle Bill" Lewis Marker—See page 54.
W. 7th Street
Chattanooga, TN 37401

Walden Hospital Marker—See Dedication.
328 E. 8th Street
Chattanooga, TN 37403

Swaim's Jail Marker
Fourth Street and Georgia Avenue
Chattanooga, Tennessee 37401

Randolph Miller Marker—See page 66.
200 E. M.L. King Blvd.
Chattanooga, TN 37403

Roland Hayes Historical Marker
E. 8th Street
Chattanooga, TN 37416

Booker T. Washington State Park Historical Marker
5801 Champion Road
Chattanooga, TN 37416

17.

YEARBOOK

This section records, highlights and commemorates some of the more memorable faces and places of the early years in Chattanooga's African American history. There are indeed many more photographs equally as deserving of the honor of being placed in this yearbook; however, in the interest of space constraints they have, regrettably, been omitted.

The Nurse Services Club, mid-1920s

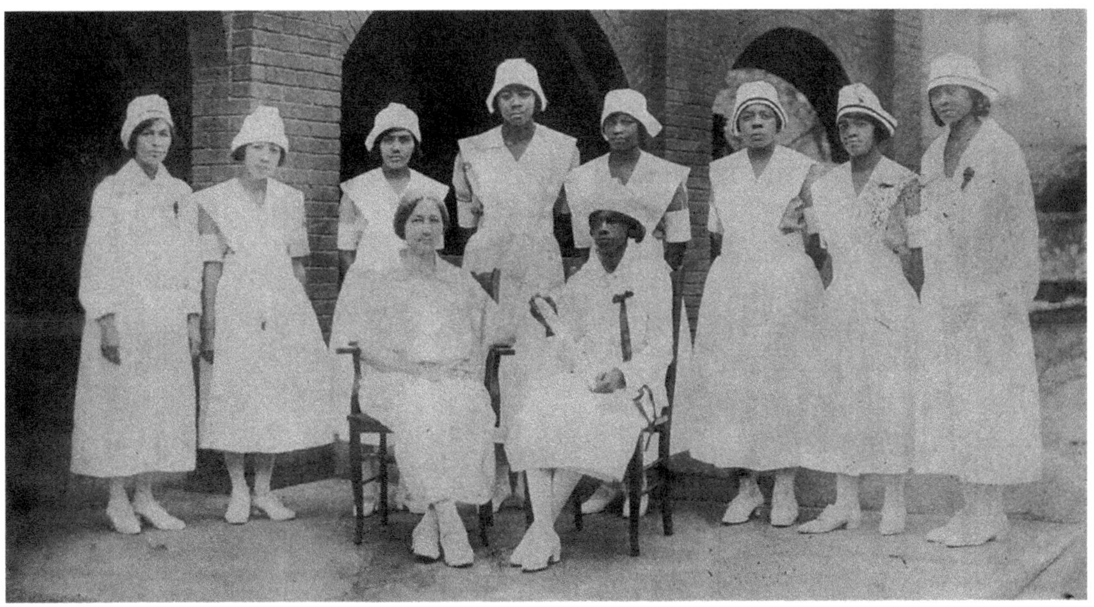

This is a photograph of the Nurse Services Club, taken sometime in the 1920s. The club was founded by Dr. Emma Rochelle Wheeler, who is seated on the left. *Photograph courtesy of Bette Wheeler-Strictland, daughter of Emma Rochelle Wheeler.*

A.M.E. Quadrennial Conference Attendees, 1904

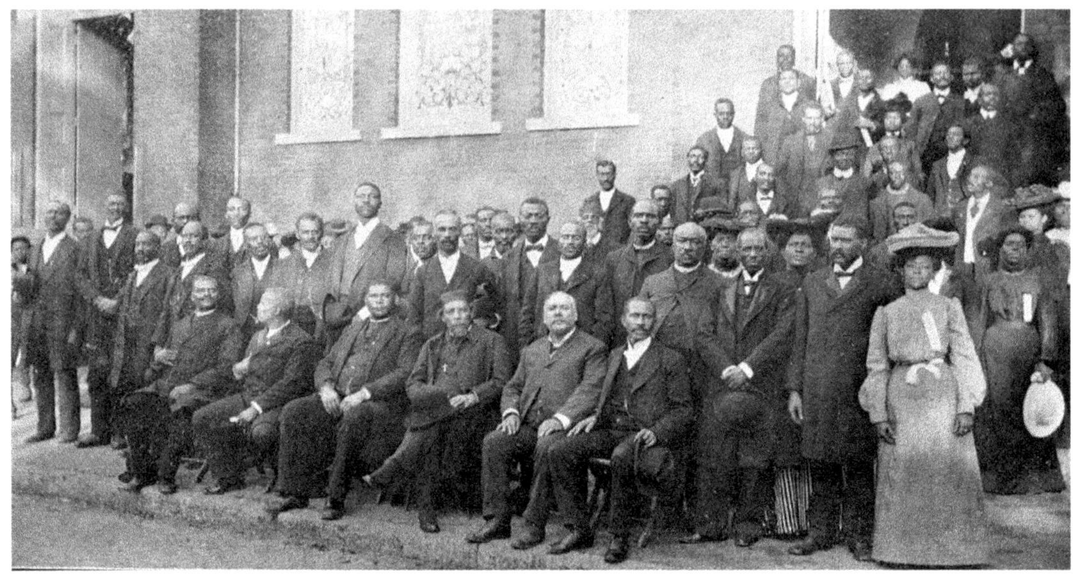

Faces from Chattanooga's African American Past: This is a 1904 photograph of the AME Quadrennial Conference attendees. *Photograph courtesy of* 1904 Biography and Achievements of the Colored Citizens of Chattanooga *by J. Bliss White.*

Hamilton County Schoolteachers, 1904

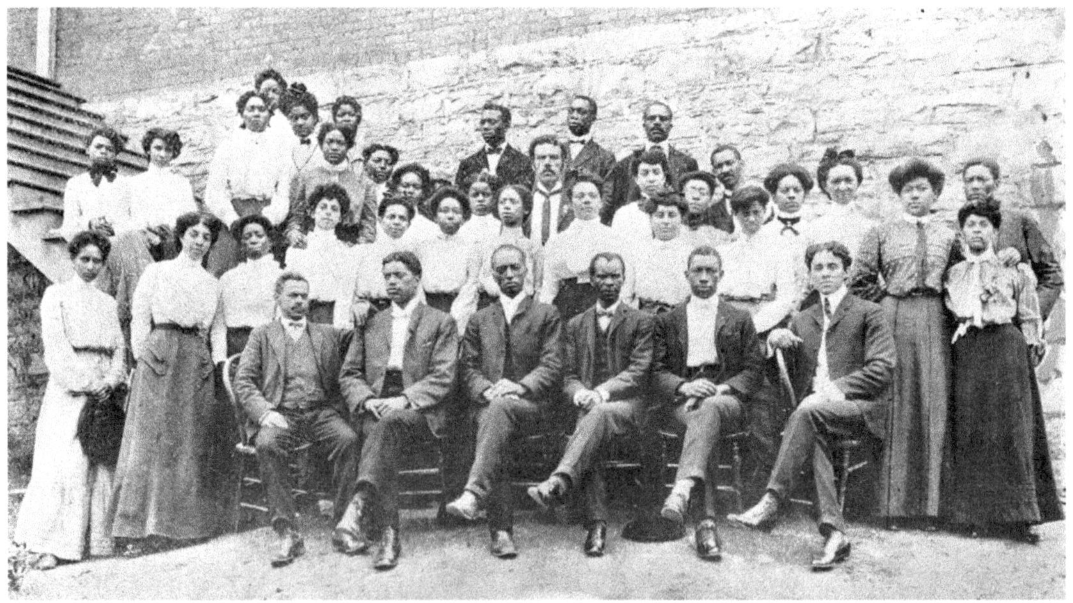

A handsome group of Hamilton County schoolteachers. *Photograph courtesy of* 1904 Biography and Achievements of the Colored Citizens of Chattanooga *by J. Bliss White*

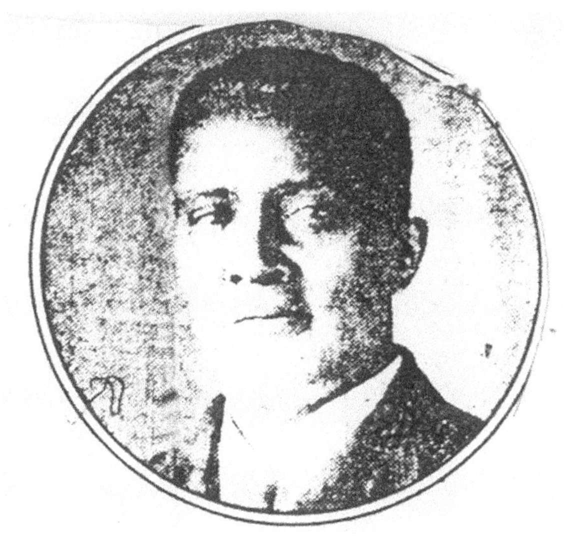

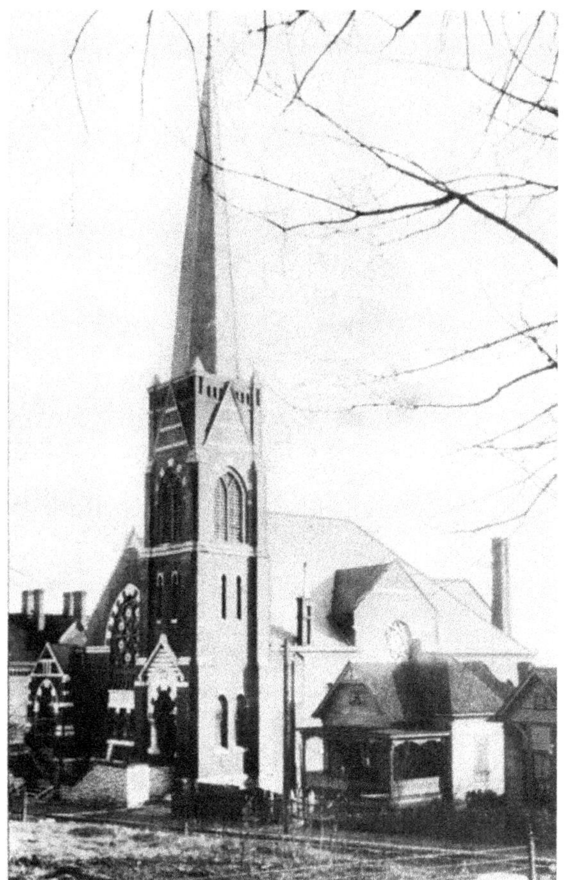

Top: A faded photograph of Mr. Charles A. Bell, who served as pastor of the First Baptist Church for over twenty years. *Photograph courtesy of the* Chattanooga Times, *July 1, 1928, Jubilee No. 25.*

Bottom: A 1904 photograph of the First Baptist Church, where Rev. G.W. Parks was pastor. According to Bette Wheeler-Strictland, daughter of Dr. Emma Rochelle Wheeler, almost all social and educational activities were held at the First Baptist Church. *Photograph courtesy of* 1904 Biography and Achievements of the Colored Citizens of Chattanooga *by J. Bliss White.*

Kirkman Technical High School

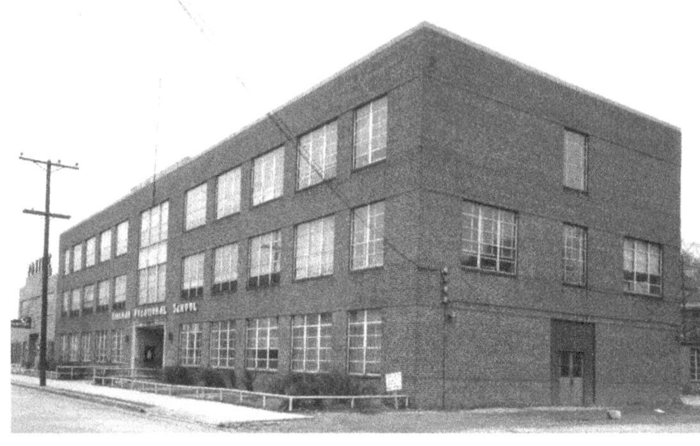

A 1943 photograph of Kirkman Technical and Vocational High School, located at 215 Chestnut Street. *Courtesy of the Paul A. Heiner Collection.*

West Main Street Elementary School

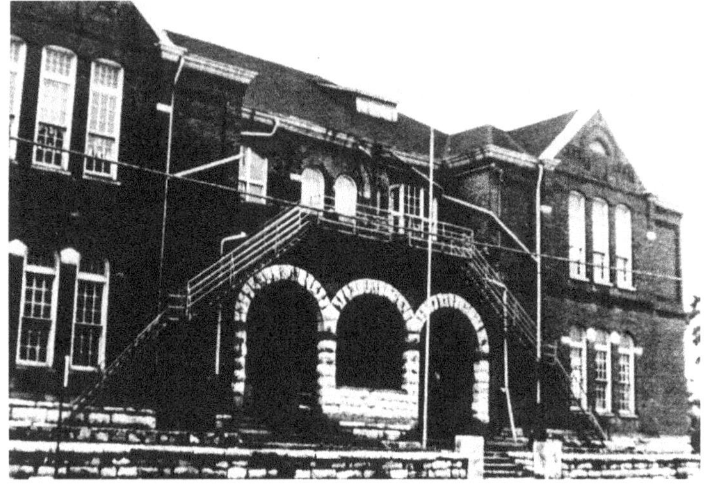

An early photograph of West Main Street School. *Courtesy of Vilma Fields and the Chattanooga African American History Museum.*

Richard Hardy Junior High

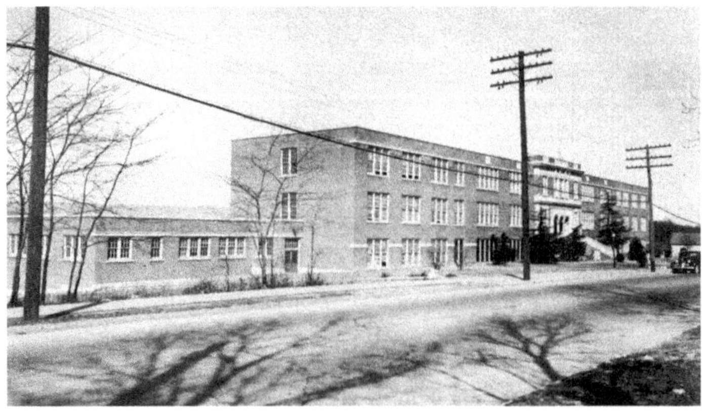

The old Richard Hardy Junior High School, which was once located on Dodson Avenue. *Photograph courtesy of* Buildings by Wilson Since 1912, *©1941 by George S. Myers and Associates.*

Appendix A

Street/Area Names, Former Street Names First

Since the time that Chattanooga, Tennessee, came into existence, its streets, roads and neighborhoods have gone through several name changes. Some streets, like Broad Street, had three names before the final name that we know in the new millennium.

The following lists are included to help the reader visualize present-day streets and areas of town that may have been called by other names in the early days. I have compiled two lists; the first includes former names first, because this is the way the names appear in the early records of the historical volume. Immediately following is the cross-referenced list (Appendix B) with present-day names first. This is not intended to be an exhaustive list.

Former Name	**Present-day Name**
A Street	Lindsay Street
Aiken Street	Eighteenth Street (18th Street)
Ann Street	Twenty-second Street (22nd Street)
B Street	Houston Street
Brabson Hill (area)	East Fifth Street (E. 5th Street)
Brannam Street	East Ninth Street (E. 9th Street)
Boyce Street	Chestnut Street
Callaway Street	Twentieth Street (20th Street)

Former Name	Present-day Name
Carolina Street (also called Caroline Street)	East Fifth Street (E. 5th Street)
Catherine Street	Seventeenth Street (17th Street)
Center Street	Twenty-fourth Street (24th Street)
Chattanooga Avenue	Twenty-eighth Street (28th Street)
Crawfish Springs (area)	Chickamauga, Georgia
Doak Street	Thirty-sixth Street
E Street	Unknown
East End Avenue	Central Avenue
Fairview Street	Thirty-ninth Street (39th Street)
Frank Street	Fourteenth Street (14th Street)
Gillespie Street	Eleventh Street (11th Street)
Gilmer Street	East Eight Street (E. 8th Street)
Hamil Road	Forty-sixth Street (46th Street)
Henry Street	Nineteenth Street (19th Street)
The Hill West of Town	Cameron Hill
Hooke	Thirteenth Street (13th Street)
Hopkins Street	Thirtieth Street
James Avenue	West Ninth Street (W. 9th Street)
John Street	Twenty-first Street (21st Street)
Johnson Pike	Ochs Highway
Leonard Street	Tenth Street (10th Street)

Former Name	**Present-day Name**
Lewis Street	Twenty-seventh Street (27th Street)
Louisa	Sixteenth Street (16th Street)
McCallie Street/Road	McCallie Avenue
Missionary Avenue	Twenty-third Street (23rd Street)
Montgomery Avenue	Main Street (also called 15th Street)
Mott Street	East Fourth Street (E. 4th Street)
Mulberry Street	Broad Street
Patten Street	Thirty-eighth Street (38th Street)
Payne Street/Battery Place	East Third Street (E. 3rd Street)
Prince Street	Thirty-third Street (33rd Street)
Railroad Avenue	Broad Street
Ruohs (Joseph) Street	Central Avenue
Stanleytown (area)	North Orchard Knob
Walter Street	First Street (1st Street)
White Street	Twenty-fifth Street (25th Street)
Whiteside Street	Broad Street
Vulcan Street	Twenty-sixth Street (26th Street)

Appendix B

Street/Area Names, Present-day Street Names First

Present-day Name	Former Name
Broad Street	Mulberry Street
Broad Street	Railroad Avenue
Broad Street	Whiteside Street
Cameron Hill	The Hill West of Town
Central Avenue	East End Avenue
Chestnut Street	Boyce Street
Chickamauga, Georgia	Crawfish Springs
Houston Street	B Street
Lindsay Street	A Street
Main Street	15th Street
Main Street	Montgomery Avenue
McCallie Avenue	McCallie Road/Street
North Orchard Knob (area)	Stanleytown (area)

Present-day Name	**Former Name**
Ochs highway	Johnson Pike
1st Street	Walter Street
E. 3rd Street	Battery Street
E. 3rd Street	Payne Place
E. 4th Street	Mott Street
E. 5th Street	Brabson Hill (area)
E. 5th Street	Carolina Street (also Caroline St.)
E. 8th Street	Gilmer Street
E. 9th Street	Brannam Street
W. 9th Street	James Avenue
10th Street	Leonard Street
11th Street	Gillespie Street
13th Street	Hooke
14th Street	Frank Street
15th Street	Main Street
16th Street	Louisa Street
17th Street	Catherine Street
18th Street	Aiken Street
19th Street	Henry Street
20th Street	Callaway Street

Present-day Name	Former Name
21st Street	John Street
22nd Street	Ann Street
23rd Street	Missionary Avenue
24th Street	Center Street
25th Street	White Street
26th Street	Vulcan Street
27th Street	Lewis Street
28th Street	Chattanooga Avenue
30th Street	Hopkins Street
33rd Street	Prince Street
36th Street	Doak Street
38th Street	Patten Street
39th Street	Fairview Street
46th Street	Hamil Road

Notes

Chapter 1

1. John Wilson, *Chattanooga's Story* (Chattanooga, TN: Chattanooga News-Free Press, 1980).
2. Diary of Dr. McCallie quoted in Zella Armstrong, *The History of Hamilton County and Chattanooga, TN* Vols. I & II (Chattanooga, TN: Lookout Pub. Co., 1940.)
3. Lester C. Lamon, *Black Tennesseans, 1900–1930* (Knoxville: University of Tennessee Press, 1977).
4. J. Bliss White, *1904 Biography and Achievements of the Colored Citizens of Chattanooga* (Signal Mountain, TN: Mountain Press, 2004).
5. Ibid.
6. Ibid.
7. Rev. W.G. Parks, "Chattanooga's Negro Population," *Chattanooga Times*, May 9, 1900.
8. James Weston Livingood, *Chattanooga: An Illustrated History* (Woodland Hills, CA: Windsor Publications, 1980).
9. The exact date of Thompson's tenure with the fire department is unknown. There was a black fire department on record in 1880 called the Carlile Unit, but Charles Walter was noted as captain.
10. *Chattanooga Times*, "Asks for a New Trial: Andy Thompson, the Well-Known Colored Politician," January 17, 1896.
11. Rev. William J. Simmons and Henry McNeal Turner, *Men of Mark: Eminent, Progressive and Rising* (Cleveland, OH: G.M. Rewell & Co., 1887).
12. Livingood, *Chattanooga.*
13. *Chattanooga Daily Times*, February 21, August 3, October 10, 12, 1900; October 15, 1902; October 11, 1905; July 11, 1937.
14. White, *1904 Biography.*
15. Wilson, *Chattanooga's Story*, 240.
16. *Chattanooga Times*, Monthly Mortuary, March 1, 1881.
17. Ibid., "The Colored Orphans [*sic*] Home," May 4, 1886.
18. Ibid., May 4, 1886.
19. Ibid., "The Steele Orphanage," May 5, 1886.

20. Ibid.
21. Mark Curriden and Leroy Phillips, *Contempt of Court: The Turn-of-the-Century Lynching That Launched A Hundred Years of Federalism* (New York, NY: Faber and Faber, 1999). Although Noah Parden would be the first African American designated as lead counsel in a Supreme Court case, he would never get to actually argue his case because a Chattanooga mob lynched his client before the case came to court.
22. White, *1904 Biography*.
23. Josephine Wheeler of New York, telephone conversation with the author, January 2004.
24. White, *1904 Biography*.
25. Wilson, *Chattanooga's Story*, 273.
26. *Chattanooga Times*, "New Negro Swimming Pool at Lincoln Park," September 18, 1938.

CHAPTER 2

27. Charles D. McGuffey, *Standard History of Chattanooga, Tennessee; with full outline of the early settlement, pioneer life, Indian history, and general and particular history of the city to the close of the year 1910* (Knoxville, TN: Crew and Dorey, 1911).
28. *Chattanooga Daily Times*, May 22, 1886.
29. Ibid., May 21, 1886.
30. *Chattanooga Times*, "Howard School," May 21, 1887.
31. Ibid.
32. Chattanooga Times, "Prof. Henry Falls Dead," February 3, 1914, 5.
33. This was the same J.W. White who was once president of the PennySavings Bank, and father of J. Bliss White.
34. This was most probably J. Bliss White, author of *1904 Biography and Achievements of the Colored Citizens of Chattanooga*. This roster appeared twenty-one years before the book came into print.

CHAPTER 3

35. White, *1904 Biography*.
36. Ibid.
37. Ibid.
38. Ibid.
39. Ibid.

CHAPTER 4

40. Wilson, *Chattanooga's Story*.
41. Lamon, *Black Tennesseans*.
42. *Chattanooga Daily Times*, July 26 and August 30, 1905.
43. White, *1904 Biography*; William Newton Hartshorn and George W. Penniman, *An Era of Progress and Promise, 1863–1910: The Religious, Moral, and Educational Development of the American Negro Since His Emancipation* (Boston, MA: Priscilla Pub. Co., 1910).

44. *Nashville American*, 1905.
45. *Chattanooga Blade*, 1905; and quoted in the *Chattanooga Times*, October 12, 1905.
46. For more information on Noah Parden, see Mark Curriden and Leroy Phillips Jr., *Contempt of Court: The Turn-of-the-Century Lynching that Launched 100 Years of Federalism* (New York, NY: Anchor Books, 1999).
47. Curriden and Phillips, *Contempt of Court*.
48. *Chattanooga Times,* "Uncle Mark Thrash, 114-Year-Old Chickamauga Resident, Plays Host to Tourists Who Come From All Parts of the Nation," January 17, 1935.
49. *Chattanooga Times*, "Mark Thrash, 122 and Ex-Slave, Talks on Nation-Wide Broadcast," May 10, 1943. Also, Stephen O. Addison, *Seen the Glory: Mark Thrash Buried the Dead at Chickamauga* (Cleveland, TN: S.O. Addison, 1991). However, a different account was written by Roscoe E. Lewis who interviewed Mark Thrash in 1959; at that time, Lewis reported that Mark Thrash said the order came from General Longstreet. Roscoe E. Lewis, "The Life of Mark Thrash," *The Phylon Quarterly* 20:4 (4th Qtr. 1959): 389–403.
50. *Chattanooga Times,* "Uncle Mark Thrash, 114-Year Old Chickamauga Resident."
51. *Chattanooga Times,* "Capt. Glenn Dies; Hurt in Accident," April 8, 1971.

Chapter 5

52. From George "Littleman" Ricks, "The History of C.D. Haslerig and Sons Dairy."

Chapter 6

53. McGuffey, *Standard History*.
54. White, *1904 Biography*.
55. November 7, 1865 U.S. Census.
56. 1880 census numbers, Geospatial and Statistical Data Center, University of Virginia Library.
57. White, *1904 Biography*.
58. Ibid.
59. Gilbert E. Govan and James Weston Livingood, *The Chattanooga Country, 1540–1976: From Tomahawks to TVA* (Knoxville: University of Tennessee Press, 1977).
60. Wilson, *Chattanooga's Story*, 277.
61. McGuffey, *Standard History*.

Chapter 7

62. Thirteenth Census of the United States, 1910, Volume I, Population, Tennessee, Table 53.
63. There were possibly more doctors. This number is taken from old newspaper articles and early histories of African Americans in Chattanooga.

CHAPTER 8

64. The Walden Hospital dedication article of July 30, 1915 did not explain this acronym, it only identified Suggs as the representative. It is known that there was a convention group called the National Court of Calanthe Delegates, who met in Chattanooga in 1904; the group was pictured in J. Bliss White's book, *1904 Biography and Achievements of the Colored Citizens of Chattanooga.*

65. *Chattanooga Times*, "Walden Hospital to Close June 30," June 14, 1953.

66. Josephine Wheeler (wife of George Wheeler and daughter-in-law of Dr. Emma Rochelle Wheeler) in telephone interview with the author, February 2004.

67. Bette Wheeler-Strictland in telephone interview with the author, Summer 2005.

68. *Chattanooga Times*, "Walden Hospital to Close June 30," June 14, 1953.

CHAPTER 9

69. Josephine Dorsey-Wheeler (granddaughter of John G. Higgins and daughter-in-law of Dr. Emma Rochelle Wheeler) in telephone conversations with the author, June 2006.

70. Simmons and Turner, *Men of Mark.*

71. *Chattanooga Times*, "Colored Exhibitors," September 3, 1895.

CHAPTER 10

72. According to the J. Bliss White manuscript, "Andrews was born in 1881, and graduated from the Pharmaceutical Department of Shaw University with the class of 1893, winning the prize for scholarship."

73. *Chattanooga Times*, "The Steele Orphanage," May 5, 1886.

CHAPTER 12

74. McGuffey, *Standard History.*

CHAPTER 15

75. White, *1904 Biography.*

Bibliography

Addison, Stephen O. *Seen the Glory: Mark Thrash Buried the Dead at Chickamauga*. Cleveland, TN: S.O. Addison, 1991.

Armstrong, Zella B. *The History of Hamilton County and Chattanooga, Tennessee.* Chattanooga, TN: Lookout Pub. Co., 1931.

Beardsley, Edward H. *A History of Neglect: Health Care for Blacks and Mill Workers in the Twentieth-Century South*. Knoxville: University of Tennessee Press, 1987.

Carney Smith, Jessie. *Notable Black American Women, Book II*. Detroit, MI: Gale Research, 1996.

Chattanooga Daily Times. Various issues.

Chattanooga News-Free Press. Various issues.

Chattanooga Observer. Various issues.

Clifton, Rob. *Chattanooga: Then and Now*. Chattanooga, TN: Rob Clifton, 2006

Curriden, Mark, and Leroy Phillips Jr. *Contempt of Court: The Turn of the Century Lynching That Launched A Hundred Years of Federalism*. New York, NY: Anchor Books, 1999.

Daily Rebel. Various issues.

Evans, E. Raymond. *Contributions By United States Colored Troops (USCT) of Chattanooga & North Georgia During The American Civil War, Reconstruction and Formation of Chattanooga.* Chickamauga, GA: B.C.M. Foster, 2003.

Fletcher, Frank. "Walden Hosptial." Chattanooga, TN: Points of Interest, June 4, 1936.

Govan, Gilbert E., and James W. Livingood. *The Chattanooga Country, 1540–1976; From Tomahawks to TVA*. Knoxville, TN: University of Tennessee Press, 1977.

Haley, James T., and Booker T. Washington. *Afro American Encyclopedia: Or, The Thoughts, Doings and Sayings of the Race*. Nashville, TN: Haley & Florida, 1895.

Hartshorn, William Newton, and George W. Penniman. *An Era of Progress and Promise, 1863–1910: The Religious, Moral, and Educational Development of the American Negro Since His Emancipation*. Boston, MA: Priscilla Pub. Co., 1910.

Heiner, Paul A. *Chattanooga Yesterday and Today*, Vols. I & II. Chattanooga, TN: Heiner Printing Company, 1960.

Howington, Arthur F. *The Treatment of Slaves and Free Blacks in the State and Local Courts of Tennessee*. New York, NY: Garland Pub., 1986.

King, Edward, and James Wells. *The Great South*. Hartford, CT: American Publishing Company, 1875.

Lamon, Lester C. *Blacks in Tennessee, 1791–1970*. Knoxville: University of Tennessee, 1981.

———. *Black Tennesseans, 1900–1930*. Knoxville: University of Tennessee, 1972.

Lewis, Roscoe E. "The Life of Mark Thrash." *Phylon Quarterly* 20:4 (4th Qtr. 1959): 389–403.

Livingood, James W. *A History of Hamilton County, Tennessee*. Memphis, TN: Memphis State University Press, 1981.

———. *Chattanooga and Hamilton County Medical Society. The Profession and Its Community*. Chattanooga, TN: The Society, 1983.

———. *Chattanooga: An Illustrated History*. Woodland Hills, CA: Windsor Publications, 1980.

Livingood, James W., with Joy B. Dunn and Charles W. Crawford, eds. *Hamilton County*. Memphis, TN: Memphis State University Press, 1981.

Lovett, Bobby L. *The Civil Rights Movement in Tennessee: A Narrative History*. Knoxville: University of Tennessee Press, 2005.

Lovett, Bobby L., and Linda T. Wynn, eds. *Profiles of African Americans in Tennessee History*. Nashville, TN: Annual Local Conference on Afro-American Culture and History, 1996.

McGenee, C. Stewart. "E.O. Tade, Freedmen's Educator, and the Failure of Reconstruction in Tennessee." *Tennessee Historical Quarterly* 63, 4 (Winter 1984): 236–238.

McGuffey, Charles D. *Standard History of Chattanooga, Tennessee; with full outline of the early settlement, pioneer life, Indian history, and general and particular history of the city to the close of the year 1910*. Knoxville, TN: Crew and Dorey, 1911.

Moore, Joanna P. *In Christ's Stead: Autobiographical Sketches*. Chicago, IL: Women's Baptist Home Mission Society, 1902.

Ochs-Oakes, George W. *Chattanooga and Hamilton County, Tenn*. Chattanooga, TN: Chattanooga Times Printing Co., 1897.

Ricks, George "Littleman." "The History of C.D. Haslerig and Sons Dairy. N.p., n.d.

Simmons, William J., and Henry McNeal Turner. *Men of Mark: Eminent, Progressive and Rising*. Cleveland, OH: G.M. Rewell & Co., 1887.

Taylor, A.A. *The Negro in Tennessee, 1865–1880*. Washington, DC: Association Publishers, 1941.

Wheeler-Strickland, Bette. Telephone and written interviews, 2003–2005. ©Rita Lorraine Hubbard.

White, J. Bliss. *1904 Biography and Achievements of the Colored Citizens of Chattanooga*. Signal Mountain, TN: Mountain Press, 2004.

Wilson, John. *Chattanooga's Story*. Chattanooga, TN: Chattanooga News-Free Press, 1980.

Wiltse, Henry W. "History of Chattanooga." MS. Chattanooga Library, ca.1900.

About the Author

Rita Lorraine Hubbard is a former special education teacher of eleven years, with a master of science degree in school psychology. She is a member of SCBWI (Society of Children's Book Writers and Illustrators) and AACBWI (African American Children's Book Writers and Illustrators), and is the author of several unpublished children's books focusing on the challenges of children in the "special" population.

Rita has two adult sons who have degrees in media arts and animation. She is also founder and CEO of Shades of Greatness™ Calendars, which pay tribute to the lives of early African American inventors. Her calendars received a favorable review from *Teaching Pre-K–8* magazine in 2004. You can visit Rita online at www.RitaHubbard.com or www.ShadesofGreatness.com.

Visit us at
www.historypress.net

www.ingramcontent.com/pod-product-compliance
Lightning Source LLC
LaVergne TN
LVHW060623110826
845147LV00015B/922

9781596293151